SILVER LLAMA

FEATHERED
BURIAL FIGURINE

Tucumán •

ATACAMA DESERT

Cerro Lhullaillaco
•

• *Cerro el Plomo*

(Santiago)

Maule River

Ecuador

Peru

INCA EMPIRE

Bolivia

0   250   500 miles

INCAS:
LORDS OF GOLD
AND GLORY

Time-Life Books is a division of Time Life Inc., a wholly owned subsidiary of
THE TIME INC. BOOK COMPANY

TIME-LIFE BOOKS

PRESIDENT: Mary N. Davis

MANAGING EDITOR: Thomas H. Flaherty
Director of Editorial Resources: Elise D. Ritter-Clough
Executive Art Director: Ellen Robling
Director of Photography and Research: John Conrad Weiser
Editorial Board: Dale M. Brown, Roberta Conlan, Laura Foreman, Lee Hassig, Jim Hicks, Blaine Marshall, Rita Thievon Mullin, Henry Woodhead
Assistant Director of Editorial Resources/Training Manager: Norma E. Shaw

PUBLISHER: Robert H. Smith

Associate Publisher: Ann M. Mirabito
Editorial Director: Russell B. Adams, Jr.
Marketing Director: Anne C. Everhart
Director of Production Services: Robert N. Carr
Production Manager: Prudence G. Harris
Supervisor of Quality Control: James King

Editorial Operations
Production: Celia Beattie
Library: Louise D. Forstall
Computer Composition: Deborah G. Tait (Manager), Monika D. Thayer, Janet Barnes Syring, Lillian Daniels
Interactive Media Specialist: Patti H. Cass

Library of Congress
Cataloging in Publication Data
Incas: Lords of gold and glory / by the editors of Time-Life Books.
    p. cm.—(Lost civilizations)
Includes bibliographical references and index.
ISBN 0-8094-9870-7 (trade)
ISBN 0-8094-9871-5 (lib. bdg.)
1. Incas.   I. Time-Life Books. II. Series.
F3429.I6   1992
980'.01—dc20   92-5149

LOST CIVILIZATIONS

SERIES EDITOR: Dale M. Brown
Series Administrator: Philip Brandt George

Editorial staff for: *Incas: Lords of Gold and Glory*
Art Director: Barbara M. Sheppard
Picture Editor: Tina S. McDowell
Text Editors: Charlotte Anker, Robert Somerville
Associate Editors/Research: Denise Dersin, Patricia Mitchell
Assistant Art Director: Bill McKenney
Writers: Darcie Conner Johnston, James M. Lynch
Senior Copy Coordinator: Anne Farr
Picture Coordinator: Gail Feinberg
Editorial Assistant: Patricia D. Whiteford

Special Contributors: Tony Allan, Ronald H. Bailey, Beryl Lieff Benderly, John Cottrell, Kenneth C. Danforth, Donald Dale Jackson, M. Linda Lee (text); Paul Edholm, Ira Gitlin, Mary Grace Mayberry, Eugenia S. Scharf (research); Roy Nanovic (index)

Correspondents: Elisabeth Kraemer-Singh (Bonn), Christine Hinze (London), Christina Lieberman (New York), Maria Vincenza Aloisi (Paris), Ann Natanson (Rome). Valuable assistance was also provided by: Gay Kavanagh (Brussels); Barbara Gevene Hertz (Copenhagen); Adriana von Hagen (Lima); Judy Aspinall (London); Trini Bandrés (Madrid); Elizabeth Brown, Katheryn White (New York); Leonora Dodsworth (Rome); Robert Kroon (Zurich).

The Consultants:
Gordon F. McEwan is associate curator and head of the Department of New World Art at the Denver Museum. He has extensive curatorial, teaching, and field research experience in ancient Peruvian archaeology, specializing in the valley of Cuzco and the origins of the Incas and their empire.

Michael E. Moseley, professor of anthropology at the University of Florida at Gainesville, provided invaluable assistance with the "Artisans of the Empire" essay in this volume. Professor Moseley has more than 25 years' experience as an active archaeologist in Peru and is the author of *The Inca and Their Ancestors*.

R. Tom Zuidema, author of numerous articles and books on Andean cultural history and a recognized expert on Huaman Poma and his chronicle, is a professor of anthropology at the University of Illinois at Urbana.

Other Publications:

ECHOES OF GLORY
THE NEW FACE OF WAR
HOW THINGS WORK
WINGS OF WAR
CREATIVE EVERYDAY COOKING
COLLECTOR'S LIBRARY OF THE UNKNOWN
CLASSICS OF WORLD WAR II
TIME-LIFE LIBRARY OF CURIOUS AND UNUSUAL FACTS
AMERICAN COUNTRY
VOYAGE THROUGH THE UNIVERSE
THE THIRD REICH
THE TIME-LIFE GARDENER'S GUIDE
MYSTERIES OF THE UNKNOWN
TIME FRAME
FIX IT YOURSELF
FITNESS, HEALTH & NUTRITION
SUCCESSFUL PARENTING
HEALTHY HOME COOKING
UNDERSTANDING COMPUTERS
LIBRARY OF NATIONS
THE ENCHANTED WORLD
THE KODAK LIBRARY OF CREATIVE PHOTOGRAPHY
GREAT MEALS IN MINUTES
THE CIVIL WAR
PLANET EARTH
COLLECTOR'S LIBRARY OF THE CIVIL WAR
THE EPIC OF FLIGHT
THE GOOD COOK
WORLD WAR II
HOME REPAIR AND IMPROVEMENT
THE OLD WEST

For information on and a full description of any of the Time-Life Books series listed above, please call 1-800-621-7026 or write:
Reader Information
Time-Life Customer Service
P.O. Box C-32068
Richmond, Virginia 23261-2068

This volume is one in a series that explores the worlds of the past, using the finds of archaeologists and other scientists to bring ancient peoples and their cultures vividly to life.

Other volumes include:

Egypt: Land of the Pharaohs
Aztecs: Reign of Blood & Splendor
Pompeii: The Vanished City

INCAS:
LORDS OF GOLD
AND GLORY

By the Editors of Time-Life Books
TIME-LIFE BOOKS, ALEXANDRIA, VIRGINIA

CONTENTS

A VIOLENT CLASH OF ALIEN CULTURES

A silver alpaca, used as a ceremonial offering, honors the woolly animal that thrived on the steep slopes of the Andes, made habitable and productive by the Incas through terracing. The giant stepped fields at Machu Picchu give eloquent testimony to the skill of the empire's engineers.

Hiram Bingham was not going to let a little bad weather stop him; still, it was not until 10 o'clock that he emerged from his tent that drizzly morning of July 24, 1911, deep in the heart of the Peruvian Andes. The night before, a local tavernkeeper—if such a name can be used to describe someone with so humble an establishment as his—had teased the explorer's imagination with a report of nearby Inca ruins. But as the tall, thin man stood inspecting the rain-swollen torrent noisily surging through the canyon of the Urubamba River, he was none too hopeful. He knew that similar reports had already led him to nothing more exciting than a few courses of ancient masonry, where some half-buried hut lay. Yet such disappointments had not deflected him from his overriding purpose—which was to find the lost city of Vilcabamba, known from historical records to be the final stronghold of the Incas. There, in semi-isolation, these proud lords of the Andes had maintained for nearly 35 years a rump kingdom in defiance of the Spaniards, vanquishers of their once-mighty empire.

Bingham had been helped in his search by a recently discovered autobiographical chronicle, dictated by one of the last Inca rulers, that provided new clues to Vilcabamba's location. His hunch was that the fabled refuge lay hidden in this densely forested valley, "designed by nature," he mused, "as a sanctuary for the oppressed."

A man of multiple interests, the 35-year-old adventurer, who taught Latin American history at Yale University, his alma mater, had come to Peru to study its history, botany, and geography. His keen enthusiasm, springing from an earlier visit to the country, had spawned the expedition he now headed, funded by Yale and some of his rich former classmates.

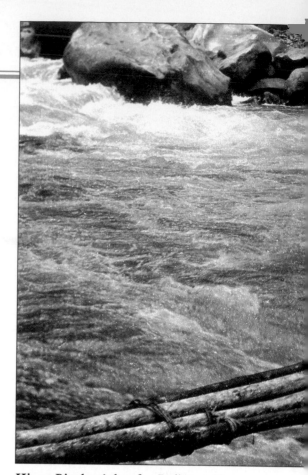

Hiram Bingham's barefoot Indian guide, Melchor Arteaga, crosses a makeshift log bridge above the turbulent Urubamba River in this photograph shot by the explorer on July 24, 1911. Moments later, Bingham himself would crawl across, terrified, on his way to the discovery of Machu Picchu, another 2,000 feet above the river valley. In his journal, he tersely noted the time, subject, and shutter speed of this, his second photograph of the day: "10:45. #2. Bridge. 1/25."

Only three weeks earlier Bingham and his team had set out from Cuzco, the ancient Inca capital, to explore the mountainous realm to the northwest, where Andean peaks soar to heights of up to 18,000 feet. The conduit here, leading from one region to the other, is the Urubamba River, which cuts a deep valley down into the dense Amazon rain forest. The area's sharply angled slopes, some of them sheer rock, and dense vegetation had discouraged travelers from straying far from its few, difficult roads. Bingham had the advantage of a new route that had been blasted along the riverbank two years previously. By traversing it, he had arrived at this wild and desolate spot, 7,000 feet above sea level. "In the variety of its charms and the power of its spell, I know of no place in the world which can compare with it," he was to write. "Not only has it great snow peaks looming above the clouds more than two miles overhead, gigantic precipices of many-colored granite rising sheer for thousands of feet above the foaming, glistening, roaring rapids; it has also, in striking contrast, orchids and tree ferns, the delectable beauty of luxurious vegetation, and the mysterious witchery of the jungle."

The explorer had listened attentively when the tavernkeeper had spoken of Inca ruins located on the saddle of an upthrusting ridge across the river from the expedition's campsite. Jotting down the names of this mountain's two peaks in his notebook—Huayna Picchu and Machu Picchu—he persuaded the reluctant tavernkeeper to lead him to the place with the promise of a silver dollar. But now, with rain falling, his colleagues—who were skeptical of the peasant's story—already had their minds set on washing shirts and perhaps hunting butterflies, and declined to go with Bingham. Thus while his teammates remained behind in the relative comfort of camp, Bingham set out in the drizzle, in the company of only the guide and a government-appointed bodyguard.

They hiked to an improvised bridge of long, spindly tree trunks, lashed together with vines, that stretched precariously across rocks in the rushing Urubamba. A single misstep and a man could fall in. "No one could live for an instant in the icy cold rapids," Bingham recalled. As his companions gingerly made their way barefoot over the bridge, Bingham got down on his hands and knees and crawled across, six inches at a time. On the opposite bank the trio mounted a steep trail, grasping vines to ascend the slippery rocks, and keeping an anxious eye out for the poisonous yellow fer-de-lance snakes known to infest the area. After climbing about 2,000 feet, they arrived at the hut of a Peruvian family. The tavern-keeper thought better about continuing, choosing instead to stay behind and gossip with the hut's owner, while Bingham and his guard continued upward, led now by a little boy not 10 years old.

After rounding a promontory and climbing a steeply terraced hillside dating from Inca times, Bingham was rewarded for his efforts. "Suddenly I found myself confronted with the walls of ruined houses built of the finest quality of Inca stonework," he was to write later. "It was hard to see them for they were partly covered with trees and moss, the growth of centuries, but in the dense shadow, hiding in bamboo thickets and tangled vines, appeared here and there walls of white granite ashlars carefully cut and exquisitely fitted together (*pages 35-45*)." Bingham could hardly believe his good fortune as he wandered among the overgrown ruins, encountering wonder after wonder—a royal mausoleum, a temple to the sun, more magnificent temples, a broad plaza, dozens of houses. "It seemed like an unbelievable dream," he exulted.

Yet was this Vilcabamba? He could not be certain. But now, his enthusiasm fired up by his find, he determined to continue his search for the lost city. The next morning the explorer broke camp, and in the course of several days of arduous trekking, stumbled upon a series of imposing ruins, including an urban site vaster in size than

9

his earlier discovery, Machu Picchu, and buried under centuries of tangled growth in an area known as Espíritu Pampa. Though it lay only 60 miles east of Machu Picchu, it was 6,000 feet lower down and difficult of access. Returning to Yale after a couple of fruitful months in the field, Bingham tentatively identified this lowlands place as his Vilcabamba, for indeed passages in the documentary evidence he had examined seemed to suggest just such a tropical location.

Yet it was Machu Picchu, nestled between the Andean peaks, that lured Bingham back for a longer stay the following year, under the joint auspices of Yale University and the National Geographic Society. Spending the summer of 1912 clearing the stone ruins, he became convinced that this picturesque citadel—and not the mysterious city buried in the jungle—was Vilcabamba, after all. Ironically, scholarly opinion now supports Bingham's original thinking.

Accessible today from Cuzco by a railway that follows the route Bingham took in 1911, the mountain retreat of Machu Picchu, built 100 years before the Spanish conquest for a ruler called Pachacuti Inca Yupanqui, has become the best-known ruin of the fabulous Inca civilization. At the apex of their power in the early 16th century, the Incas, an aristocracy of a few thousand individuals, all members of a single ethnic group, ruled one of the largest empires of the era. Their territory stretched for more than 2,500 miles down almost the entire length of the Andes, from the southern border of

En route to Machu Picchu in 1911, Hiram Bingham poses with his mule. Among his belongings he carried a leatherbound notebook (above), in which he scribbled the details of his adventure: the weather and topography, his impressions of each of the retreat's stone edifices, a crude map of the site—and the sequence in which he took his photographs, the first ever to be shot of the forgotten city, made with a Kodak 4 x 5 camera (right).

today's Colombia to what is today Santiago, Chile, incorporating all of present-day Ecuador and Peru as well as parts of Bolivia and northwest Argentina. Its heartland lay on the precipitous spine of the Andes, the world's second-highest mountain range after the Himalayas. Its eastern boundaries touched the rain forest of the Amazon headwaters and its western, the sands of the bleak coastal deserts. The Incas called this domain Tahuantinsuyu, the "land of the four quarters," a name reflecting the segments into which the empire was officially divided, with Cuzco at its center. Within it—and very much under the Incas' thumb—lived an estimated seven to nine million people comprising as many as 100 ethnic groups.

Defying conventional assumptions about what made highly developed civilizations possible, the extraordinary Incas succeeded without benefit of wheeled transport or writing. Through sheer will power and the application of their keen intelligence to the harnessing of human energy, they created in less than 100 years one of the most intricately organized societies the world has known. But the meteoric rise of the Incas was followed by their even more precipitous fall. Tahuantinsuyu was ruled by a succession of great warrior-kings, each of whom was known, in his reign, as the Sapa Inca, the "sole Inca" or "unique one." Extending their rule over an expanding territory, these monarchs gained a prestige that led their subjects to accord them the exalted title Son of Inti—Inti being the Inca sun god—as well as the deference and riches due such status.

Yet for all its power, this imposing civilization was conquered in short order by fewer than 200 Spaniards. The invaders' courage and even their advanced weaponry might have amounted to little against so formidable and numerous a foe had events been different.

But it was the Incas' fate that the Spaniards would be aided in their victory by events taking place within the empire itself.

Rumors of a land of gold had long been circulating among Spaniards in the New World in the early 16th century, and hearsay evidence indicated that it lay somewhere south of the equator. Tempted by such talk, a veteran of Spain's Italian campaigns named Francisco Pizarro decided to find out the truth for himself. Illegitimate and illiterate, he had come to the New World in 1502 to seek his fortune. He saw seven years' hard service in the Caribbean, where he helped suppress the Taino Indians on the island of Hispaniola, today's Dominican Republic and Haiti. In 1513 he accompanied Vasco Núñez de Balboa across the Isthmus of Panama to become one of the first Europeans to behold the Pacific Ocean. Settling down in Panama, he became a landowner, was given a quota of Indian workers, and grew to be quite well-off. But such success left him restless. Joining forces with Diego de Almagro, another soldier of fortune, and Hernando de Luque, a priest, they put together an expedition that in 1524 would take them from Panama on a difficult and frustrating journey into the unexplored territory to the south.

A second expedition launched in 1526, on which Pizarro bartered for gold, provided enough of a glimpse of riches to inspire him with dreams of wealth and glory. One of his ships captured a group of Inca traders on a raft of balsa wood borne by sails of finely woven cotton. The Spaniards shrewdly held three of the captives to be trained as interpreters, setting the others free. "They were carrying many pieces of silver and gold as personal ornaments," Pizarro later reported to his emperor, Charles V, and he went on to whet the ruler's appetite by listing some of the items—among them, "crowns and diadems, belts and bracelets, armor for the legs and breastplates; tweezers and rattles and strings and clusters of beads and rubies."

This expedition was even more arduous than the first, leading many of his men to despair as hunger, disease, and death overtook them. But Pizarro would not be deterred by adversity. He pulled out his sword and drew a line in the sand. "Comrades and friends," he said, pointing to one side, "there lies the part that represents death, hardship, hunger, nakedness, rains, and abandonment; this side represents comfort. Here, you return to Panama to be poor; there, you may go on to Peru to be rich. Choose which becomes you as good Spaniards." Thirteen elected to remain with their leader, and for this they came to be known as "the 13 of glory."

As is revealed by this schematic map based on Bingham's hypothetical identification of sites, terraces fall away from the spine of the Andes, where a grassy plaza divides Machu Picchu into two wards. The city gate (1) permits entrance at the southern end, near the Sacred Plaza temples (2) and the intihuatana (3), the large stone where Incas worshiped the sun god. The palace known as the King's Group (4) and the temple called El Torreón (5) are among the finest of the 200 or so stone buildings, which also include clusters of small houses (6), so-called prisons (7), and storehouses (8). Huayna Picchu looms at the city's northern edge.

In 1527, Pizarro reached the Inca town of Tumbes. There the Spaniards were greeted with friendly curiosity by the town's inhabitants, who told them of temples inland, sheathed in precious metals, and of gardens where living plants grew alongside finely crafted replicas of gold and silver. Such accounts further stoked Pizarro's desire. Lacking neither the manpower nor the resources to attempt an immediate invasion of Inca territory, he determined to return at the head of a conquering force in the near future. But despite the lure of riches to come, it would take three years and a trip to Spain before all the necessary arrangements could be made.

In his home country, Pizarro had proudly told Charles V of his discoveries and of the Inca treasure that could be theirs for the taking. Excited by the prospect of territorial and financial gain, Charles bestowed on the adventurer the right to explore and conquer this hitherto unknown empire on the other side of the world. Pizarro was to have the title of governor and captain-general in the lands that came under his control. As would soon become apparent to Pizarro and his cohorts, the delay in setting out, frustrating though it had been, actually worked to their advantage.

The story of the Incas' tragic downfall is known mainly from the reports of the Spaniards. With the notable exception of Pizarro, the conquistadors—among whose ranks was Hernando de Soto—had a high degree of literacy, and the records they left behind offer eyewitness descriptions of the first encounters between the two civilizations. Once the conquest was accomplished, other, more sympathetic, recorders followed, who used the knowledge they gleaned from the Incas themselves to describe Inca traditions. From both sets of accounts and the observations of conscientious civil servants sent to the new colony by Spanish rulers, ethnohistorians have been able to piece together a picture of the Incas during their last days. It is a sad one.

Embroiled in a fierce battle against each other for the supreme position of Sapa Inca, royal brothers Huascar (above, left) and Atahualpa—illustrated in watercolors from a 16th-century Spanish album—plunged the Inca empire into chaos. Arriving in the thick of the civil war in 1532, the conquistadors exploited their enmity—and ultimately annihilated the civilization. The Spaniards believed their actions were "to the glory of God, because we have conquered and brought to our holy Catholic faith so vast a number of heathens, aided by His holy guidance."

In 1524, when the empire of the Incas was at the height of its glory, rumors arrived at the Sapa Inca's court of extraordinary events. "Floating fortresses" had sailed along the northern coast bearing strangers with white skin and hair on their faces, who came to be called "the bearded ones." The news was disturbing to many; in later years, Inca nobles told a Spanish chronicler that the Sapa Inca himself, a great warrior named Huayna Capac, had seen the danger and foretold that one day the strangers would threaten his throne.

Within a year or two the Sapa Inca was dead. Although it is impossible to verify the disease that carried him off, it seems likely that it was smallpox, introduced to the Americas by the conquistadors. Outpacing the conquerors, this illness reached native peoples even in lands the Spaniards had yet to explore and probably arrived in western South America by 1525, from the Caribbean via Venezuela and Colombia, where the Europeans already had a foothold. The disease spread so quickly among the Incas, who had no immunity to it, that armies were decimated and entire families stricken. It has been said of smallpox that a cup of water offered at the right moment can save a life, but often there was no one well enough to provide the dying a drink. Morale plummeted among survivors, most

Driven by lust for gold and dreams of glory, the Spanish adventurer Francisco Pizarro—shown in battle regalia in this 19th-century painting—conquered and looted the rich Inca empire with an army of fewer than 200 men. In 1541, at the age of 63, he was stabbed to death by supporters of his one-time ally, Diego de Almagro, whom Pizarro's brother Hernando had executed after the two rivals warred for supremacy of Peru.

of whom had lost numerous relatives and friends. Not only did the epidemic kill Huayna Capac; it also carried off his probable heir, setting the stage for strife.

It was customary for the Sapa Inca to nominate his successor. Although the honor normally devolved on one of the sons of his principal wife, the Coya, it was not necessarily the eldest who was chosen, but rather the one considered most fit to rule. A new Sapa Inca, Huascar—whose name, "gentle hummingbird," should not be taken as a reflection of either his character or his stature—was proclaimed successor in Cuzco by the Inca nobles there.

Much of the court was not in Cuzco, however, but in the northern city of Quito, which Huayna Capac had conquered, and where he had elected to spend the latter years of his life. It was there that trouble began. Quito had become almost a second capital, splitting the hitherto united leaders of the empire into two contending factions. The army, which was quartered in Quito, preferred another son of Huayna Capac, Atahualpa—whose name means wild turkey cock, a bird that commanded respect in the Andes. He had more than proved himself, having spent most of his life at his father's side in the field of battle.

One Spanish veteran described Atahualpa as being "of fine person, of medium size, not too fat, beautiful of face and grave, with red eyes, a man much feared by his people." As evidence of the impact his bearing had on people, this observer described seeing an important nobleman "tremble in such a manner that he could not stand upon his feet" in the royal presence for fear he may have displeased the ruler. The dread was not entirely irrational; Atahualpa could be ruthless. He also showed a quick intelligence that impressed the Spaniards, who noted how quickly he became an expert at chess.

Although he had repeatedly proclaimed his loyalty to the new Sapa Inca, Atahualpa knew that Huascar must view him as a rival. Alert to the possibility that one of his brother's supporters might try to assassinate him if he left his power base in Quito, he ignored every effort to persuade him to come to Cuzco to pay his respects. For five uneasy years a standoff endured. Finally, Huascar brought events to a head by demanding his brother's presence. When Atahualpa again failed to appear, sending ambassadors bearing gifts in his place, Huascar—egged on by courtiers hostile to his brother—had the emissaries tortured and killed, then sent an army to bring Atahualpa to Cuzco by force. Angered, Atahualpa called his faction to arms, and the land—already mourning the loss of so many of its citizens to the smallpox epidemic—soon found itself in the throes of a civil war.

It was a blood-drenched conflict with no quarter given, and it set in motion the process of destruction that European invasion would subsequently complete. At first Huascar's men were successful, and Atahualpa was captured. He escaped, however, and joined his army. Meeting his former captors in battle, Atahualpa defeated them; following Inca military custom, he had the skull of the opposing commander, another brother, lined with gold and turned into a drinking vessel, and his skin made into a drum. Huascar dispatched a second army; but his raw troops proved no match for the veterans surrounding Atahualpa, and, in a two-day battle, they were defeated.

Now it was Atahualpa's turn to take the offensive. His generals marched south toward Cuzco. They met a third royal army recruited to protect the city. This time Huascar's men seized the initiative; they set brush fires that broke up the enemy lines and drove the soldiers from the field. Regrouping, Atahualpa's generals prepared an ambush in a ravine near the battlefield. It netted the greatest prize of all—Huascar himself, captured alive. His army was subsequently routed, and Atahualpa's men entered Cuzco in triumph.

They showed no mercy to the defeated enemy. Tied to a frame, Huascar was forced to watch while his numerous wives were butchered. His friends and advisers were also slaughtered, and their remains left tied to poles lining a road out of the city as a bloody warning of the danger of thwarting Atahualpa's will. Huascar was held prisoner in the fortress of Jauja, there to await his fate.

It was during this period of upheaval, in 1532, that Pizarro and Almagro, who had accompanied him on the two previous expeditions, returned to the town of Tumbes. This time Pizarro had with him some 160 adventurers, 67 of whom were horsemen, and an assortment of weapons, including muskets, crossbows, pikes, lances, and artillery, supplied by Charles V. He found not the prosperous city he had earlier visited but a devastated ruin; like much of the Inca empire, it had suffered grievously in the course of the civil war and had been ravaged by smallpox. While the sight disheartened Pizarro's men, their commander was shrewd enough to realize that the Indians' misfortune could be the Spaniards' gain. Lingering for five months near the coast, sustained in part by the looting of the em-

This skull—probably the remains of a defeated opponent—may once have been lined with gold and used for chicha, *a beer most often brewed from corn. Such skull cups served as symbols of victory for Inca leaders who triumphed in battle.*

peror's storehouses there, Pizarro sought to find out what he could about the state of Inca affairs. When news came that Atahualpa was encamped at Cajamarca, less than a fortnight's march away from him, he set off into the interior with his tiny army, a few Indian lackeys, and two Indian translators whom he had taken from the raft some years previously.

It was a desperate, almost mad enterprise. Indeed, nine of Pizarro's men, daunted by the prospect of entering the mountainous domain of the Inca, turned back. The rest of the little band pressed forward, climbing ever higher, crossing raging torrents on perilously narrow suspension bridges made of ropes of ichu grass slung from stone pilasters. They could not help being impressed by the evidence of Inca engineering skills all around them, including flagstone-paved roads, bordered with shade-giving trees, with water running in stone channels alongside for the convenience of travelers. "Such magnificent roads can be seen nowhere in Christendom, in country as rough as this," one of them conceded.

While the Spaniards pursued their arduous upward trek, the thin air of the heights making it harder and harder for them to breathe, the victorious Atahualpa was resting with his army at Cajamarca, favored by Inca rulers for its healthful hot springs. Earlier he had received word that the bearded white men, whose advent had troubled his father, had returned in their wooden ships. Soon runners from the coast informed him that the strangers were moving inland. Atahualpa responded by sending an envoy to invite Pizarro and his men to visit him. The report the Inca ambassador carried back to his master contained the first of a series of fatal misreadings of Spanish intentions. As Atahualpa later revealed, the emissary told him the bearded ones were not fighting men, and that 200 Incas would be sufficient to restrain them, if indeed they posed a threat. The Inca could not have known that Pizarro had fostered such an assessment by receiving the ambassador in a courtly manner, giving him a shirt and two goblets of Venetian glass, and talking of peace. Consequently, the little army of strangers was allowed to march unmolested through the mountains.

The Spaniards panted in their armor up tracks that clung vertiginously to soaring mountainsides. Forced to dismount by the steepness of the ascent, the troopers led their horses, weighted down with cannons, armaments, and supplies, along paths so narrow that a single false step could have sent men and beasts plunging to their death down condor-haunted ravines. They found the commanding heights dominated menacingly by stone fortresses, which, to the exhausted soldiers' relief, turned out to be unmanned.

After a week in the mountains, Pizarro's army descended upon the valley of Cajamarca on November 15, only to be greeted by an alarming sight. According to one eyewitness, so numerous were the Inca warriors scattered on the hillside "that we were filled with fright. We never thought the Indians could occupy such a proud position, nor so many tents, so well set up. It filled all us Spaniards with confusion and fear. But we dared not show it, much less turn back, for if they sensed the least weakness in us, the very Indians we brought with us would have killed us."

Pizarro quartered his men in the main square, an open space surrounded on three sides by long buildings, each with several doors. He dispatched a group of horsemen led by Hernando de Soto to pay his respects to Atahualpa and to lure him to a meeting. Tense but resolute, the Spanish envoys rode through the silent ranks of the Inca army along a paved road to the royal residence, located near the hot springs a few miles from the town. In the courtyard of the royal palace, "a pool had been made, and two pipes of water, one hot and one cold, entered it; the two pipes came from springs," one of the men later reported. There they found the new ruler sitting on a golden stool, "with all the majesty in the world, surrounded by all his women and with many chiefs near him."

A war of nerves was played out between the two parties. Atahualpa had sought to impress Pizarro with the military might at his command, and he had succeeded. The Spaniards, too, tried to disconcert their opponents. Understanding how remarkable horses seemed to the Indians, who themselves had no domestic animals larger than llamas, de Soto charged straight at Atahualpa, then pulled up his mount so close to him that the tasseled fringe the monarch wore as a crown was stirred by its breath, while froth from its mouth dripped on his clothing. But Atahualpa sat immobile, a perfect model of the Inca warrior in the face of danger. He expected similar fortitude from his followers; those who flinched he later had executed.

Atahualpa remained silent for a while, then addressed the newcomers through one of the interpreters they had brought with them. He chided the Spaniards for having robbed his storehouses of

EXPLORER GENE SAVOY AND THE LOST CITIES OF THE ANDES

Often hidden out of sight, covered by jungle, or perched on distant peaks, seemingly well beyond reach, some—but not all—of the lost cities of the ancient Andean peoples have revealed themselves to a few hearty individuals with the patience, fortitude, and wherewithal to go look for them. The American explorer Gene Savoy *(below)* is one such person, and in the three decades that he has been trekking through the Andes, he has found more than 40 previously unknown settlements that tell excitingly of the societies that built them, then vanished.

Savoy had long been fascinated by Vilcabamba, the last stronghold of the Incas. Attempts to locate it had not been successful. As far back as 1834, the French Count de Sartiges endured weeks of exhaustion and thirst searching for the ruins. Other intrepid souls followed, each, in turn, certain he had found the elusive city. In 1912, Hiram Bingham joined the ranks when he declared Machu Picchu to be the Incas' final refuge. Although for the next 50 years most scholars accepted his claim, not everyone was convinced. On the heels of a failed attempt by a 1963 American team that parachuted deep into unexplored jungle, Gene Savoy set out for the most likely site, one, ironically, that Bingham had stumbled on but dismissed, 93 miles northwest of Cuzco.

Savoy had prepared himself well, having carefully studied historical chronicles for clues, gotten the backing of the Peruvian government, and assembled a support team. After days of struggling through the thick vegetation of mountain rain forests, Savoy and his men came upon the city at last. "We couldn't believe our eyes," he remembers. The ruins, situated between two

Gene Savoy, head of the Andean Explorers Foundation and Ocean Sailing Club, is shown here en route to Gran Vilaya, a forgotten city he found in Peru's forbidding Chachapoyas region. The map inset at right, which was drafted by his team's own cartographer, details the area of discovery.

rivers on a flat alluvial plain covered by trees and vines, occupied an area of approximately two square miles.

Not an archaeologist, Savoy would leave the digging to others. And soon he had set his sights on a search for another lost city, one he would call Gran Vilaya. "I was sure of one thing," Savoy writes. "Something did exist in the eastern jungles, but no one had managed to find it." At Vilcabamba, he had seen circular buildings that he believed were the work of the Chachapoyas, a people who had inhabited the northernmost reaches of Peru. Their domain, some 500 miles northwest of Vilcabamba, lay 8,000 to 10,000 feet above sea level in cloud-wreathed mountains and dense rain forest. The region was so remote that the Incas supposedly added the kingdom to their empire only in 1480, taking, it is thought, 40 years to subdue the inhabitants. With its suffocating jungle growth, almost perpetual rain, and lack of human habitation, the area had deterred archaeologists for decades.

In 1965, Savoy's team traced by air Inca roads leading from Vilcabamba into the Chachapoyas kingdom. It took a preliminary expedition days to locate the first ruins, 9,400 feet above sea level. Savoy named this site Gran Pajatén, after the famous colonial ruins of Pajatén nearby. There the team explored a complex of slate-and-mortar circular structures, many of which were covered with mosaic-like stone figures of humans, animals, and birds, apparently condors (*background*).

One day, while flying in a helicopter, Savoy and some of his teammates spotted caves in cliff faces relatively close to Gran Pajatén. Amazingly, three-foot-high wood carvings, found in the caves, were still in fine condition, despite centuries of exposure to the humidity. As a follow-up, a ground-survey team pursued Inca roads 90 miles northwest and came upon dozens of cliff tombs with mummy cases

Gran Pajatén's main circular structure, shown at left, stands on a platform and measures 45 feet in diameter and about 12 feet in height. Its facade is divided in half by a molding, and its upper sections are covered with geometrical friezes. Roots and vines wrapped around the ornamental stonework threaten to topple the giant structure, which perhaps may once have been a temple.

Gran Pajatén's imposing ruins are composed of thousands of individual stones fitted compactly together like those shown above. The human figures on the left are made from long black slate blocks. One head is crowned with sunburstlike rays; the other two have wings.

standing in rows inside the caves *(background)*. Some had been shot down by looters, and the shattered casings and their spilled contents of bone and textile lay on the earth below. Suspecting that this was a Chachapoyas necropolis, Savoy named the site Pueblo de los Muertos—City of the Dead. Systematic exploration revealed seven similar sites within a 40-square-mile area.

Abandoning the Chachapoyas region for more accessible areas, Savoy would not return for 15 years. This time he was determined to find the administrative center of the Chachapoyas, mentioned by Spanish chroniclers, and accompanied by almost 100 machete men, 70 mules, and 20 crew

members, he did. It turned out to be a collection of linked settlements sprawling through 100 square miles of rain forest alive with the sound of monkeys and parrots. Over the next five years, he led eight expeditions into the area, exploring thousands of architectural remains that were perched on some 40 major mountaintops, with the peaks connected by broken roads. Among the ruins were what may well have been administrative buildings, temples, dwellings, and a network of

ridge-top fortifications. "Gran Vilaya," says Savoy, who named the site after a nearby river canyon, may prove to be "the largest pre-Columbian city of the Americas. Its ruins dwarf Cuzco and everything the Incas ever built."

Gran Vilaya is certainly Savoy's most spectacular find and has been a magnet to archaeologists, who hope eventually to solve its many mysteries. As to what else may lie out there in the jungles, still awaiting discovery, Savoy has a ready answer: "Plenty."

These anthropomorphic mummy cases were once decorated with paints in vivid colors. Made with mud and vegetable fiber, the cases are believed to contain the remains of rulers.

At Diablo Huasi, just south of Pueblo de los Muertos, dozens of tombs mark the cliff face. One cave contained numerous mummies with their knees drawn up to their chests, wrapped in a netlike material, and surrounded by grave goods. As is their policy, Savoy's group left the cave undisturbed for the archaeologists.

Gran Vilaya is made up of thousands of white limestone structures like these. The buildings, many of which stand on terraces, range up to 40 feet in height and between 25 to 30 feet in diameter.

"some of my father's cloth" on entering the country and for having treated several of his chiefs badly. The conquistadors responded by boasting of their prowess as soldiers, disparaging some coastal Indians with whom they had actually fought for behaving "like women," and adding that one horse would have been enough to conquer their "entire land." But, cagily, the Spaniards also offered to apply their military acumen on behalf of Atahualpa. Before the brief encounter came to an end, Atahualpa, in his second tragic misjudgment, agreed to come to Cajamarca the next day to visit Pizarro.

That night was an anxious one for the Spaniards. Gazing out over the Inca campfires, "as thick as the stars of heaven," in the words of one soldier, they realized there was no turning back. Throughout the night they prayed and confessed their sins to their priests.

The two camps lay in wait for dawn, each led by a veteran warrior seeking personal legitimacy within the empire he served. Atahualpa wanted most of all to be officially crowned god-king of the Incas, thereby eliminating the challenge of his imprisoned half brother. The humbly born Pizarro, for his part, hoped that by becoming governor of Spain's newest colony he would at last attain prestige and acclaim. Each, on the morrow, would face a decisive encounter with an alien world. Pizarro, however, had an advantage: For years, he had dealt with peoples of the New World, studying their strengths and weaknesses. And his lessons in conquest had come from the master himself when, in Spain, he had listened to Hernán Cortés, his cousin, tell the story of how he had wrested Mexico from the Aztecs. Atahualpa, while able to muster hundreds of thousands of fierce, battle-hardened fighters, knew nothing of the European character.

At this key moment Pizarro decisively stamped the mark of his leadership on his forces. Uncouth and callous though he may have been, no one ever accused him of lacking courage. It has been reported that he was pleased by his men's desperation, which he deemed a welcome spur to the fighting he envisaged. "Make fortresses of your hearts, for you have no other," he told them. Based on the example of Cortés, who had conquered the mighty Aztec empire by kidnapping its emperor, he prepared an ambush.

Meanwhile, Atahualpa was plotting his own military strategy. Overnight, he sent 5,000 soldiers under command of his general, Rumiñavi, to seal off the road north of Cajamarca. His plan, he later told the Spaniards, was to take Pizarro and his men alive and sacrifice them to Inti, the sun god, retaining their horses for breeding. At dawn the next day, Pizarro stationed his forces within the buildings around the square to await Atahualpa's arrival. As morning turned to afternoon, the waiting told on the nerves of the massively outnumbered soldiers. Later, one recorded, "I have heard that many of the Spaniards made water without knowing it out of sheer terror."

Finally, at sunset, the imperial cortege approached. It seems that Atahualpa chose the time believing that the Spaniards were unable to ride horses in the dark. He provided a magnificent spectacle, and an intimidating one. On a wooden litter, lined with multicolored parrot feathers and decorated with jewel-encrusted silver and gold plates, Atahualpa was carried aloft by 80 retainers dressed in blue tunics, their badge of honor. Wearing a collar of emeralds over a robe woven with golden threads, the monarch held a gold shield emblazoned with an image of the sun.

"All the Indians wore gold and silver disks like crowns on their heads," one awed Spaniard later recorded. "In front was a squadron of Indians wearing a livery of checkered colors like a chessboard." Musicians played flutes, drums, and conch-shell trumpets to accompany dancers and choral groups who, as they marched, sang a song of praise to Atahualpa: "O great and very powerful Lord, Son of the Sun, only ruler, may all the earth obey you." One Spaniard recalled that it was "by no means lacking in grace for us who heard it." But another soldier remembered that it "sounded like the songs of hell."

Atahualpa had left the body of his army—some 80,000 men—outside the town, but his personal retinue nonetheless comprised upward of 5,000 warriors. Amazingly, they arrived unarmed, in ceremonial rather than in military array. Entering the square, they found it empty but for the odd figure of a robed Dominican friar, bearing a cross in one hand and a Bible in the other. The royal council in Spain had specified that heathens should be given the chance to accept Christianity voluntarily before there was any recourse to bloodshed, and the conquistadors were eager not to break the letter of the law. As the friar expounded the Christian faith to the bemused ruler, the translator told him that he was being asked to convert to the religion of the strangers. "You say your god was put to death, but my god," Atahualpa replied, pointing to the setting sun, "still lives."

He took the missal handed to him, at first showing interest in the writing it contained. He understood that it was believed by the

Spaniards to be what the Incas called a *huaca,* a talisman in which resided the spirit of the gods. Yet it may have seemed a flimsy token compared with the great stone huacas the Incas worshiped, and he dismissed it, throwing it to the ground. "This says nothing to me," he said contemptuously. The friar turned to Pizarro and is reputed to have said to him and his men: "Throw yourselves upon them forthwith. I give you all absolution."

Pizarro gave the signal for the attack. Two cannons fired into the massed Indians. The Spanish horsemen charged out of the buildings in their armor, cutting a swath through the ranks of unarmed men. The foot soldiers followed to the sound of blaring trumpets, rending the air with their battle cry of "Santiago," the name of the saint who the Spaniards believed aided them in battle.

The focus of the attack was Atahualpa himself. His nobles sought to protect him, but, unfamiliar with the sharpness of honed steel, many lost their hands to the slice of swords as they struggled vainly to keep the litter high in the air. The Spaniards turned the square and the surrounding plain into a killing field, and only their leader's intervention saved Atahualpa, as Pizarro roared above the din, "Let no one wound the Indian upon pain of death!" He then dragged Atahualpa into a building, there to be held under guard. Meanwhile, the massacre continued unabated. In the two hours before darkness fell, 6,000 Inca troops died in and around Cajamarca, yet not a single Spaniard was killed. Among the few to be wounded was Pizarro, slightly injured accidentally by one of his own men as he struggled to take his royal prisoner alive. "It was not accomplished by our own forces," one Spaniard commented afterward, "for there were so few of us. It was by the grace of God, which is great."

From that moment on, the Spaniards were the effective masters of the Inca empire, and nothing would ever be the same again. Commentators have since tried to understand why Atahualpa made the deadly error of marching unarmed into Cajamarca. Perhaps he was deceived by the blandishments of the Spaniards, who had spoken to him only of friendship and alliances. And when he heard from his spies that the bearded ones were huddling inside the buildings of the town, it probably suggested to him not ambush but cowardice.

Given the overwhelming numbers of his troops, Atahualpa had apparently not even considered the possibility that Pizarro's paltry force of fewer than 200 men would attempt to assault him, amid his vast army, in the heart of his empire. His lack of insight into

A POWERFUL FIGHTING FORCE WITH A BRONZE AGE ARSENAL

Because of the sheer manpower they could muster—often hundreds of thousands strong—and their impressive arsenal of short- and long-range weapons, the Incas had the most formidable

MACE HEAD

armed force in South America, before the advent of the Spaniards.

Theirs was primarily a citizen army. All able-bodied men between the ages of 25 and 50 were subject to be drafted for up to five years. Each province supplied both rank and file and officers. At the bottom of the hierarchy, every 10 warriors formed a group, headed by a leader responsible for supplies and discipline. The next level of command was of five such groups, and two five-group units were placed under the dictate of a still-higher officer. Leadership thus rose in a pyra-

mid to the commander in chief, the Sapa Inca.

This highly organized force was backed by an efficient communications and supply system. The Incas could move soldiers over thousands of miles of roads, dotted with storehouses stocked with food, clothing, and a variety of bronze weapons. Of these arms the sling, or *huaraca (below)*, was often the first employed, since fighting usually began at a distance. The soldier would slip an egg-sized stone into the middle of the fabric. After twirling the belt

MACE WITH AX

above his head, he would release one end, propelling the missile toward an opponent as far as 30 yards away.

Drawing closer, the warrior used a javelin. And in hand-to-hand combat, he might swing a rope, at the end of which flew a spiked copper mace *(upper left)* that he would

BOLA

slam into his foe's skull. Alternately, fighters employed star-shaped clubs, with copper, bronze, or stone heads fastened to wooden handles, sometimes with an ax blade attached *(center)*.

When the Spaniards invaded the Andes, their horses, swords, and firearms offered new targets. Adapting their tactics, the Incas relied more heavily on the bola *(upper right)*, three stones attached to lengths of llama tendons. The device was spun in the air and then launched toward the enemy. Entangling their legs, it brought mounts and men crashing to the ground.

SLINGS

27

the invaders' mentality gave him no inkling of the confidence Pizarro and his men derived from their feeling of superiority to all peoples of the New World, whom they saw as heathens. They drew courage from the conviction that on their side was God, the powerful empire of Charles V, and the unrelenting forward thrust of European civilization. The Incas had harbored a similar faith in their destiny, but the smallpox epidemic and the civil war had done much to shake it.

On hearing of Atahualpa's capture and the massacre of so many of his troops, the general in charge, Rumiñavi, fled, with his men, north to Quito. The other two veteran generals were in Cuzco. Atahualpa himself was eager to keep his own forces at bay, fearing that the Spaniards would kill him if they were attacked by Incas.

In captivity, Atahualpa was allowed to maintain the trappings of a king. His women and servants lived in the closely guarded quarters assigned him, and his people still came to him for their orders, which were scrupulously obeyed. He knew, therefore, all that was happening within the empire and could transmit to his officials, when he wished, secret instructions. Within the space of 20 days, he learned to speak Spanish and also to read a little, an achievement that went beyond that of the illiterate Pizarro.

Shrewdly observing the glint that gold brought to the eyes of the bearded ones, Atahualpa resolved to buy them off by promising them history's most spectacular ransom. He agreed to fill the room in which he was being held—a chamber 22 feet long by 17 feet wide—with gold, piled up as far as he could reach above his head. He also said that he would fill a hut "twice over with silver."

When the Spaniards first heard Atahualpa's remarkable offer, they thought he was joking, but soon became convinced that his intentions were genuine. After Pizarro had a legal paper drawn up documenting this proposal, they sat back to wait while the treasure was brought to them. It began arriving by the llama-load—tumblers, vases, and finely wrought ornaments, including an idol the size of a

Of the vast amount of precious metalwork crafted in the Inca empire, only a few pieces remain, such as the 10-inch-long gold sculpture of seven seabirds shown above left. Almost all were melted down into ingots and shipped back to Spain to pay its mounting debt—and to be made into such extravagances as this gold-leaf altarpiece in the cathedral at Seville.

four-year-old child, as well as 700 plaques of gold stripped from the walls of temples in Cuzco, where they had been mounted over stone. These were thrown in pell-mell, along with delicately wrought models of plants and animals, even a fountain spouting a solid jet of gold with golden birds and animals playing in the pool below. One observer reported that he saw 200 loads of gold arrive from Cuzco, each on a litter supported by four bearers, while one litter was so weighed down with precious metal 12 people had to carry it.

Despite making good on his offer, Atahualpa had effectively signed his death warrant, again in a miscalculation of his adversaries. To the Incas, gold had little intrinsic worth. They called it the "sweat of the sun" (silver was the "tears of the moon") and saw the glittering metal as being aesthetically pleasing and hallowed, to be fashioned into beautiful objects or statues of gods to adorn holy places. They respected labor and put far more value on their extraordinary weavings, each cloth representing thousands of hours spent at the loom. These fabrics, rather than bullion, were the real currency of the empire. It was hardly likely, therefore, that Atahualpa could have comprehended the depth of European gold lust. Sending out orders to empty Cuzco of its treasures, he little imagined that nothing less than the entire wealth of the empire would satisfy the Spaniards. Atahualpa worried instead that the captive Huascar might offer the bearded ones an even larger amount of gold to purchase his own freedom. So he sent secret orders to his generals to kill his half brother, who perished with his wife and his mother; their bodies, it was said, were cut to pieces.

The last act of Atahualpa's tragedy was played out before the Spaniards left Cajamarca. Word of the empire's riches had filtered out of the country, attracting newcomers eager for a share of the loot. But to safeguard the treasure for themselves, Pizarro and his followers had agreed that the ransom would be divided up among them as the price for their courage, the lion's share going to the men who had been present at Atahualpa's capture. The gold alone, when melted down, came to 13,400 pounds, and the silver weighed even more— 26,000 pounds. Since any booty seized while Atahualpa was still alive could be construed as part of the ransom, the late arrivals were eager to dispose of him in order to win their portion of future pickings. They spread the rumor that Atahualpa was plotting an assault by the Inca army to rescue him, which struck fear in the hearts of the outnumbered Spaniards. Atahualpa, realizing that a plot was afoot,

The foundations of one of three towers at the fortified temple of Sacsahuaman, scene of Inca resistance, reveal how it was constructed in triple stone circles. The outermost ring has a diameter of 75 feet.

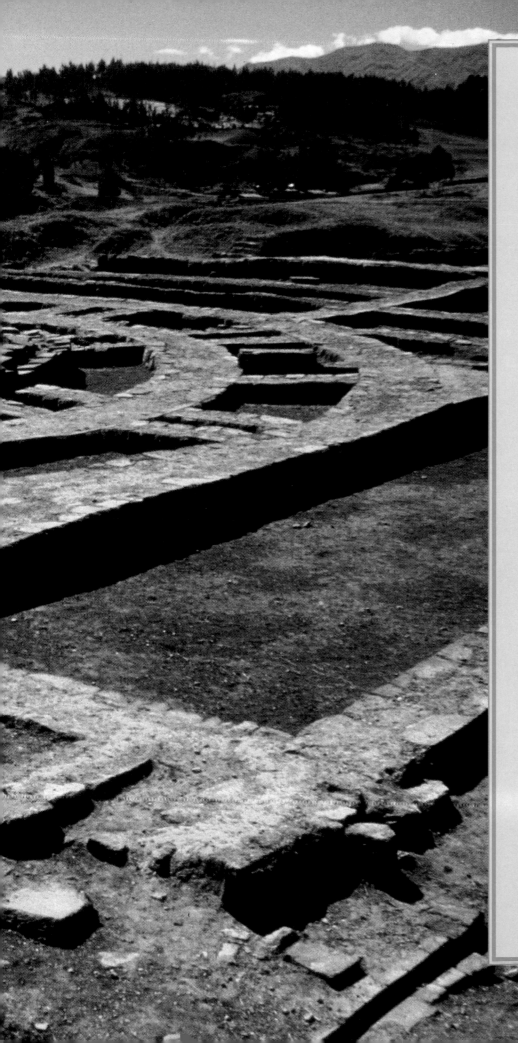

HAUNTING RUINS OF INCA DEFEAT

In an attempt to regain control over their destiny, some 100,000 Incas besieged 190 Spaniards and their supporters within Cuzco in 1536. As part of their strategy, they hurled red-hot stones at the city's thatched roofs, setting them afire and nearly suffocating the enemy. Trapped, many of the desperate Spaniards asked their leaders to abandon the city, but a decision was made to fight back.

The Inca attacks on Cuzco came mainly from the massive hillside fortified temple of Sacsahuaman *(left)*. The Spaniards launched a 50-horse cavalry charge on the stronghold, withstanding showers of javelins and stone missiles lobbed from slingshots. By late afternoon, Juan Pizarro, Francisco's brother and the leader of the assault, received a mortal blow. The following day, the Inca ruler, Manco Inca, sent 5,000 reinforcements. The Spaniards then resorted to European siege tactics, scaling the walls and eventually driving the defenders into the fort's towers. Supplies there ran low. Still, resistance continued for several days more. Although the Spaniards had won Sacsahuaman, the Incas under Manco kept up their own siege of the city, which went on for a year. Perhaps because of the arrival of Spanish reinforcements or a lack of will on the part of his men, Manco retreated to the wild areas northwest of Cuzco to launch further resistance from there. But the Incas' fate had already been sealed.

now reconciled himself to death and shifted his attention to a noble objective—immortality. The Christian version held no meaning for him, but within his own religion the Sapa Inca was guaranteed life everlasting if his body was properly mummified, and to this end Atahualpa directed his final efforts.

Pizarro tried to restrain his men from taking hasty action against his prisoner, but eventually he was panicked into agreeing to the Inca's execution. Contemporary accounts record that there was no trial other than a meeting of Pizarro's council, who agreed that Atahualpa should be burned alive. He wept when told of his fate, for the destruction of his body would deny him immortality. "What have I or my children done to merit such a fate?" he asked Pizarro.

Tied to the stake, he listened while a friar made a last effort at conversion. Realizing that if he were baptized, he would be garroted rather than burned, he agreed to these rites, assuming that his body would be turned over to his people for mummification. In a final betrayal, after strangling him, the Spaniards burned part of his body and clothing. Then they buried him, as one grumbled, "with as much pomp as if he had been the most important Spaniard in our camp."

For all his suspicions of Atahualpa, Pizarro was not blind to the advantage of having a native ruler under Spanish control as a way of ensuring the obedience of the peoples of the far-flung empire. His choice, Manco Inca, a surviving son of Huayna Capac, who had supported Huascar against Atahualpa, was popular with the people of Cuzco, the stronghold of the Huascar faction. Still, these Cuzco residents took no chances; before the Spaniards entered their city, they took care to hide—not their gold but their most precious possessions, the mummies of former emperors. When Pizarro's men arrived, many welcomed them as restorers of the legitimate Inca line.

The Incas soon saw how mistaken they had been. When they had conquered neighboring peoples, they had normally allowed the local chiefs to retain their dignity as well as their titles so long as they agreed to rule alongside the Inca governors. But the conquistadors proved much less generous. They abused Manco and showed no regard for Inca customs. Worse

In fierce defiance of their conquerors, traditionally armed Inca warriors battle Spanish soldiers. Inca resistance, depicted on this wooden kero from postconquest Peru, continued from 1532 until 1572 when Viceroy Toledo called for the use of "fire and blood" against the Inca empire's last stronghold, Vilcabamba.

was to come when Pizarro quit Cuzco for the coast to found a new capital, Lima. He left his younger brother, Gonzalo, in charge, with another brother, Juan, to assist him. Gonzalo treated Manco with undisguised contempt, even abducting and raping his favorite wife.

With reports of Spanish atrocities flooding in from around the empire, the previously pliable Manco balked at further compliance. He attempted to escape from Cuzco, but was captured and brought back in chains. Placed in jail, he was subjected to further humiliations by his captors, who, he later claimed, urinated on him and burned his eyelashes with candles. From that time on there was no longer any question of accommodation with the Spaniards.

Soon after Gonzalo departed on a mission of reprisal for the murder of several of his countrymen, Manco persuaded Hernando Pizarro, another of Francisco's brothers, who had recently come to Cuzco from Spain, to release him so that he might pray at a shrine where there was a golden effigy of his father. He said that he wanted to present the statue to Hernando as a gift, and apparently the Spaniard believed him. Once out of Cuzco, Manco called on his people to revolt. At last they had a champion to lead them against the invaders, and, in the tens of thousands, they flocked to join him. In a moment of triumph that validated the Inca organizational genius, warriors were recruited, fed, and transported to the outskirts of Cuzco, without alerting the Spaniards to their movements. Alarming news reached Francisco Pizarro in his new city: Cuzco was under siege.

The siege was to last for almost a year, during which the Inca capital was effectively cut off from the rest of the country. A fierce, two-week battle for control of the fortresslike temple of Sacsahuaman was won by the Spaniards. During the siege Indian collaborators in and around Cuzco had sneaked food to the Spaniards. These traitors included some of Manco's own relatives, who, like others, feared retaliation for their earlier support of the Europeans if Manco gained the upper hand. The siege failed when Spanish reinforcements arrived. Manco's followers saw that their best opportunity was gone, and most drifted away.

The results of the conquest for the peoples of the Inca empire were terrible indeed. The shock of defeat was more than they could bear, and many lost their will to live as the empire deteriorated all around them. Estimates suggest that the population of Tahuantinsuyu may have been reduced by three-quarters in the half-century after the arrival of the Spaniards, from perhaps seven million to about

HITCHING POST OF THE SUN

Winding away from the Sacred Plaza and up a terraced granite outcrop, a long stairway charts a dramatic climb to a carved, polygonal stone at the summit—the *intihuatana,* or "hitching post of the sun," in its colorful translation. (*Inti* means sun; *huata,* to tie.) Here, Bingham hypothesized, the Incas may have symbolically tethered the sun to prevent it from straying away at the winter sol-

stice. "The priests," he wrote, "able, on the twenty-first or twenty-second of June, to stop its flight and tie it to a stone pillar in one of their temples, were regarded with veneration."

The elegant stone, sculpted from the mountain itself, may have served as a solar observatory, allowing priests to determine the best times for sowing and harvesting crops by noting the disappear-

ance of its shadow at the spring and fall equinoxes. On these occasions, the priests would have decked the stone with great quantities of flowers and herbs. In particular, during the Inti Raymi—the magnificent sun festivals held in June and December—the residents of Machu Picchu probably gathered at the intihuatana for days of harmonious chanting, effigy rituals, and prayers.

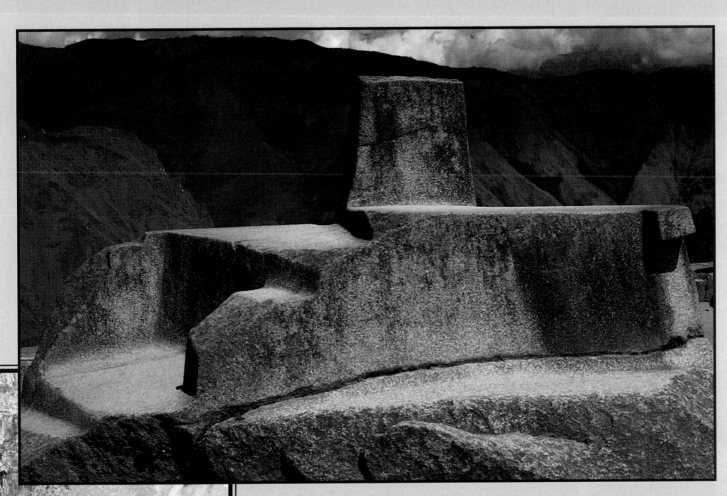

Jutting almost six feet from the ground, the monumental intihuatana—carved from the granite bedrock—is the tallest Inca monument of its kind still in existence. Apparently the Inca sculptor cut away only those portions of the stone that did not possess huaca, or holy aspect.

Surrounded by jungle growth, Bingham's escort, Sergeant Carrasco, places his hand on the stone, the so-called intihuatana, most likely used by the Incas for worship of the sun god, Inti. Beside him stands the anonymous farmer's son who guided Bingham and Carrasco into the ruins.

Spreading over the Andean spine, the excavated terraces and granite buildings of Machu Picchu resemble a "patterned blanket thrown over a great rock," in the words of Yale University art historian George Kubler. The city's beauty lies in its remarkable integration of architecture and environment.

AN EMPIRE BUILT BY A MAN CALLED EARTHSHAKER

Taking advantage of a pleasant Sunday afternoon in May 1950, about a third of Cuzco's residents, some 15,000 people, had flocked to the outskirts of the Peruvian town for a soccer match. Others had gone to church, or were strolling the cobbled streets, when, in a sudden lacerating shudder, an earthquake ripped apart the city, toppling buildings and leaving 83 people dead beneath the debris. Although the cataclysm shook the city for only seconds, its political tremors continued to ripple through Cuzco's social structure for six years as the 400-year-old domination of the Indian past by Spanish culture was dislodged.

Many of the buildings erected by the Spaniards on the ruins of the Inca capital collapsed under the earthquake's impact, and the narrow old streets were strewn with granite blocks that to one witness looked like nothing so much as "big black dice." As in earlier quakes, however, most of the oldest stone foundations of Cuzco withstood the fierce seismic blows. These were the finely crafted walls that the Incas had painstakingly fitted together without benefit of mortar, five centuries before, in creating what the conquistador Pedro Sancho conceded was a city "so large and so beautiful that it would be remarkable even in Spain."

Near the center of Cuzco, under the rubble of the 16th-century church of Santo Domingo and a portion of its monastery, a

Found near the body of a boy who was probably sacrificed to the sun god, this silver figurine clad in parrot feathers and luxurious vicuna wool may represent a deity intended as the child's escort into the next world.

magnificent 20-foot-high curved retaining wall of dark gray andesite remained intact, as did the complex's other Inca stonework. And to the wonder and delight of many, the earthquake had laid bare additional stretches of imposing Inca walls previously hidden by the colonial structures.

These splendid walls, upon which Dominican friars had first built their church and monastery, once belonged to the holiest shrine in the Inca empire: the Temple of the Sun, dedicated to Inti, the supreme deity. The Incas called this compound of a half-dozen buildings the Coricancha, the "golden enclosure." Here, alongside an effigy of Inti himself, they had placed the idols of the peoples they had subjugated. Daily rituals honoring the god were performed in the main temple—and in other temples modeled on the Coricancha throughout the realm—by the high priests and the cloistered women whom the Spaniards had memorably dubbed Virgins of the Sun. At the break of each day, Inti's devotees threw to the rising sun a ceremonial kiss, known as the *mocha*.

The Spaniards were dazzled by the Coricancha. The chronicler Pedro de Cieza de León declared Inti's temple to be "among the richest in gold and silver to be found anywhere in the world." He described how "halfway up the wall ran a stripe of gold two handspans wide and four fingers thick. The gateway and doors were covered with sheets of this metal. There was an image of the sun, of great size, made of gold, beautifully wrought and set with many precious stones. There was a garden in which the earth was lumps of fine gold, and it was cunningly planted with stalks of corn that were of gold—stalk, leaves, and ears."

A bountiful harvest of gold and silver from the Coricancha helped pay Atahualpa's ransom after he was taken prisoner by the conquistadors. The Spaniards stripped 700 gold plates from the walls alone—"like boards from chests," noted Pizarro's secretary. When melted down, each plaque yielded an ingot of four and a half pounds. Having plundered its riches, the conquerors turned the shell of the Coricancha over to the Dominicans, the powerful religious order that had administered the brutal Spanish Inquisition.

Even in its denuded state the Coricancha was impressive, and though much altered over the centuries, it became a lure to scholars probing its secrets. In the late 19th century, the friars permitted the American diplomat and archaeologist Ephraim George Squier to, as he said, "ransack every portion of the church, and every nook and

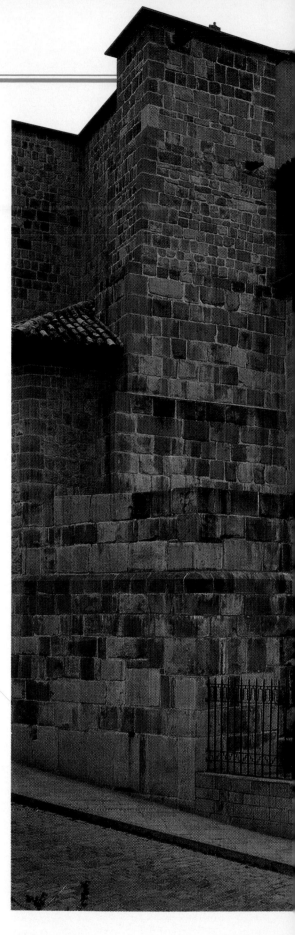

corner of the convent, and to measure and sketch and photograph to my fill. Here a long reach of massive wall, yonder a fragment, now a corner, next a doorway, and anon a terrace—through the aid of these I was able to make up a ground plan of the ancient edifice." In 1928, the German archaeologist Max Uhle discovered previously hidden remnants of the original Inca structure beneath a side altar. Then, in the 1940s, the archaeologist John H. Rowe of the University of California pored over the monastery and mapped out a general floor plan, which was largely validated when hidden portions of the Inca structures came to light in 1950.

Earthquakes had forced the Dominicans to rebuild their church several times over the centuries. But after the extensive damage of 1950, an unprecedented public outcry on behalf of the older structures compelled restorers to grapple with a dilemma their predecessors had not faced: Which ruins should be saved—the Spanish colonial church or the Inca temple? A team of advisers sent to Cuzco in 1951 by UNESCO (United Nations Educational, Scientific, and Cultural Organization) resisted local pleas in favor of the temple and recommended restoration of the church, citing its value as a beautiful and important example of early colonial architecture. But public pressure mounted to preserve the monuments of Peru's Inca civilization at the expense of its Spanish heritage. By the time Peruvian architects began serious restoration six years later, planners had decided to ignore UNESCO's recommendation and give priority

Symbolizing the clash of two cultures, the reconstructed Spanish church of Santo Domingo sits atop its Inca foundation, the curved wall of the Temple of the Sun, at Cuzco. Built during the reign of Pachacuti from perfectly fitted blocks of dark igneous rock, the sacred wall of the Coricancha—"golden enclosure"— has withstood centuries of earthquakes, while the colonial structure above it has crumbled and been repaired many times over.

to the Inca ruins. Since then, several sections of the church and monastery have been removed to reveal part of the labyrinth of walls once sheathed in gold, revered by the Incas as the "sweat of the sun."

It was only fitting that this small triumph on behalf of the vanquished Incas should have occurred in Cuzco. Lodged in a valley on the western slopes of the snowcapped Andes 11,000 feet above sea level, the city had been the political, religious, and ceremonial core of the Inca world, possessing, according to the chronicler Cieza de León, an "air of nobility." Cuzco began humbly, one of several small farmers' villages in the valley, and perhaps would have languished as such had not the hero Inca Yupanqui risen to power there less than a century before the Spanish conquest. Possessed by a vision of Inca supremacy, this skillful military man and brilliant political organizer managed, in scarcely more than three decades, to expand his little domain into Tahuantinsuyu, "land of the four quarters," a realm that in its size and efficiency rivaled the Roman Empire at its height. The royal name he chose for himself was, appropriately enough, Pachacuti—which means cataclysm or earthshaker.

Under Pachacuti, perhaps the greatest leader produced in ancient America, and his son, Topa Inca Yupanqui, the Incas subdued every major state and tribe in the Andean region, thus creating not only the largest empire in the pre-Columbian New World but also the most carefully planned and administered one. They applied their remarkable organizational ability with a fervor that captivated the Spanish conquerors almost as much as did their gold. Indeed, so effective were they that, like the old walls of Cuzco, many of their ideas and practices survive today among the populations of the countries their empire once encompassed.

As illustrated in the diagram above, the ancient Inca capital of Cuzco was designed in the shape of a puma, holy symbol of strength and power; the outline is still visible at the heart of the modern-day city (opposite). Ramparts at the puma's head (1) held the fortified temple complex of Sacsahuaman; royal palaces and administrative and religious buildings surrounded a huge plaza set in the puma's midsection (2); and noble families made their homes in the Puma Chupan, or puma's tail (3), an area located at the point where two rivers that had been turned into canals flow together.

Because the Incas lacked writing and could not set down in words their formidable accomplishments, they present modern scholars with the difficult problem of sorting fact from legend. Much of what is known about the earliest Incas has come from stories passed from one generation to another by the people. European travelers and missionaries often blended the tales they heard into their descriptions of the empire. Thus the surviving record is a colorful mix of truth and legend, tinged, in some instances, by Inca propaganda.

Still in its infancy, Peruvian archaeology has been struggling both to correct the ambiguities and misinterpretations and to verify the accuracy of the old accounts. Considered one of the most reliable of the Spanish chroniclers is Pedro de Cieza de León, who for 17 years roamed about the empire as a common soldier. Though he viewed the Incas through the lens of a different culture—and that of a conqueror to boot—he proved a careful listener and a keen observer. Another important chronicler, El Inca Garcilaso de la Vega, was the son of an Inca princess and a Spanish soldier; he knew the indigenous customs and language. But his status as a half-caste held in inferior regard by the Spaniards led him to extol, on occasion, the virtues of his mother's heritage at the expense of the truth.

As far as can be determined from the patchy historical record, the Incas date back to about AD 1200. That much is known from a chronological list of their rulers. They descended from a small ethnic group of highlanders living in the Cuzco valley, but the details of their early existence soon fade into myth. The word *Inca* did not even appear in the Incas' own oral histories until mention of the sixth ruler, who adopted the title Sapa Inca. Only later did these mountain dwellers themselves come to be known as Incas.

According to the legends still learned by Peruvian schoolchildren, the founder of Cuzco was Manco Capac, the first ruler. He and his people, as one myth has it, emerged from one of three caves at Paccaritambo, 18 miles to the southwest. Other myths have Manco appearing on an island in Lake Titicaca, much farther to the south. At Cuzco, say the legends, Manco plunged a golden staff into the ground where the glittering Coricancha would rise. The fertile earth swallowed the rod, thus signifying its acceptance.

The ancient stories establish the Incas as the children of the sun god, Inti, who entrusted·them with the task of taming and educating the savages they encountered. But however blessed they may have been, their ascent to greatness was slow, in part because they gained supremacy initially through intermarriage with other groups in the Cuzco valley. Over the course of two centuries, the Incas managed to subdue some of their neighbors, expanding their realm within the perimeter of a dozen or so miles around Cuzco.

The Incas did not begin to fulfill their true destiny until the emergence of their ninth ruler, Pachacuti. He could not have had a more inauspicious start as a young man: He was just one of the many sons of the eighth ruler; indeed, his brother, Urcon, had already been named successor by their father. Pachacuti might have languished in the background had he not been called to his life's work by Inti in a vision, which, if nothing else, suggests the vast scope of the prince's early ambition. According to a story told to Father Bernabé Cobo, a 17th-century Jesuit missionary, Inti appeared to Pachacuti with snakes coiling around his arms. "Upon seeing this image," recounted Cobo, "Pachacuti became so terrified that he started to flee." The sun god reassured him: "Come here, my child, have no fear, for I am your father the sun. I know that you will subjugate many nations and take great care to honor me and remember me in your sacrifices."

Inti then revealed to him by means of a magic crystal images of all the regions Pachacuti would conquer. But it took a military crisis to give the young prince the opportunity he needed. In 1438, Cuzco came under threat of attack by a powerful force of warriors known as the Chancas. The danger was so great that Pachacuti's aging father, Viracocha Inca, and Urcon, the heir apparent, fled to a mountain fortress, taking along with them their best soldiers.

Whether powered by his vision or goaded by a desire to show up Urcon—or both—Pachacuti refused to leave. As the Chancas prepared to storm Cuzco, he took charge. To augment his own few troops, he drew men from neighboring tribes. When the Chancas opened their assault at dawn, Pachacuti was ready. Clad in the skin of a puma, an animal that the Incas regarded as the embodiment of strength and power, he led the counterattack. At the critical moment, say the legends, he summoned supernatural aid. The very stones on the battlefield turned into warriors, and their ghostly ranks helped repel the enemy. Cuzco was safe.

Pachacuti now forced his father to abdicate and took the throne. He then went on to a series of other military triumphs. With an army composed of men from other conquered tribes but officered solely by Incas, he gradually extended his dominion north into the central Peruvian highlands and then south to the shores of Lake Titicaca. As the Spanish-Inca chronicler Garcilaso put it, "A prince's thirst for conquest, like his ambition, increases with his power."

But Pachacuti had a vision of the future. Warfare in the past had been largely a matter of looting and then withdrawing to the home territory. He used war differently—not just to acquire diverse resources but also to spread Inca culture and religion. He knew that the Incas were regarded by their enemies as formidable foes. They traditionally embarked upon new campaigns singing the grisly victory song that, too often, became literal truth: "From his skull we shall drink. We shall adorn ourselves with his teeth. His bones will serve as our flutes. With his skin for a drum, we shall dance." Yet Pachacuti also knew that, to achieve victory, it might suffice merely to strike terror in his enemies, rather than to actually engage them in combat. He would send emissaries to a foe preaching the advantages of surrender. Spanish chronicles tell how he would invite his adversaries "in the name of the Sun to acknowledge his authority,

Found near
Lake Titica
royal garb:
coloring of c
It probably
llama, symb
the first llam
larly sacrifice
especially dur

ELEGANT ARTISTRY WITH THE SIMPLEST TOOLS

Scouring the ancient quarry for clues to Inca building practices, Protzen, a Swiss, discovered numerous river cobbles—egg-shaped rocks weighing from more than 20 to less than 2 pounds with pit marks on their smaller ends, a good indication they had been used for pounding. He took up one of the heavier rocks and hammered a chunk of raw stone into a rough rectangle, then dressed the sides and squared the edges with smaller cobbles. Protzen was sur-prised to discover that "the process can be repeated for a long period, and the effort required is small."

From existing Inca walls, he knew that the blocks in each row have concave top faces. Protzen pounded a similar depression into the top of another large stone, then laid the convex side of his own block on top, leaving an imprint in the fine dust raised by his pounding. In some places the dust was compressed, indicating an improper fit. Through repeated pounding and fitting, he was able to match the blocks exactly.

But another mystery remains. Many of the large blocks bear protrusions, called *jetas*. Protzen suggests that these knobs may have facilitated lifting the blocks during the fitting process. But other experts point out that many jetas are sized and positioned in ways that would make them of no use as building aids. More likely, the jetas had a mystical rather than a practical function.

Stone steps and a massive retaining wall at the Sacsahuaman bastion exemplify the Incas' penchant for lofty design. The rounded cornerstones have a graceful, almost pillowy look despite their immense size, while the beveled joints cast deep shadows in the bright Andean sunshine.

A classic example of polygonal construction—randomly shaped blocks fitted together like pieces in a jigsaw puzzle—this wall in Cuzco includes one stone with 12 angled sides. The block nestles so tightly against its neighbors that a knife cannot penetrate the joints between them.

This elegant doorway lies below the Temple of the Sun at Ollantaytambo. The surrounding wall embodies the culmination of the polygonal style. Its blocks bear many of the enigmatic jetas, whose purpose remains shrouded in doubt.

Set in a wall of coursed masonry—smooth, symmetrical blocks in perfectly straight rows—this trapezoidal wall niche in Cuzco's Coricancha (golden enclosure) represents some of the finest Inca stonework. Tiny holes in the niche's frame were used for affixing gold plates, which adorned the temple in great quantities.

HARMONY OF STRUCTURE AND ENVIRONMENT

While few traces remain of the crude mud dwellings that housed the vast majority of the population, there exist ruins of upper-class domiciles and imperial administrative centers that demonstrate how Inca architecture reflected the diverse environments of the Andean region.

Along the empire's arid coast, scarce rainfall allowed adobe to predominate and roofs to be laid flat. The only feature that distinguishes Inca buildings here from earlier or later construction is the ubiquitous use of trapezoid-shaped doors and niches.

In this temperate zone, the conventional pattern of the cancha—the residential compound—evolved. The cancha consisted of living quarters and storage buildings grouped around a central courtyard. When this layout was transferred to the wetter, colder, windy highlands, the courtyard was retained, but the roofs acquired gables for deflecting rain, and stone supplanted adobe.

Examples of state-sponsored construction of the time done under bureaucratic auspices also reflect climatic considerations and a certain uniformity of style.

These desolate walls mark the site of a cancha not far from Machu Picchu belonging to a member of the Inca elite. The buildings are of the stone-and-mud-mortar construction called pirca, *the most common form of Inca masonry. The stone gables once supported steeply pitched, thatched roofs to facilitate rainwater runoff in this wet climate.*

Perched on a hillside at Ollantaytambo, this complex of buildings is thought to have been either a storehouse for the area's inhabitants or barracks for an Inca garrison. Staggered one above the other, each building commands breathtaking views of the Urubamba valley from numerous large windows. Individually, the buildings impart a light and airy aspect. As a whole, the cluster merges naturally into the slope and seems altogether appropriate for its mountain setting.

Flanked by sturdy walls, the royal retreat at Pisac—only a small segment of which is shown here—exhibits coursed masonry of red volcanic stone. The semicircular wall (center) is the ruin of the palace's Temple of the Sun. Terraces surrounding the central buildings were put under cultivation, mostly for growing corn, and also served to hinder an enemy's approach. Commissioned by Pachacuti, Pisac's design suggests it functioned as a fortress as well as an imperial residence.

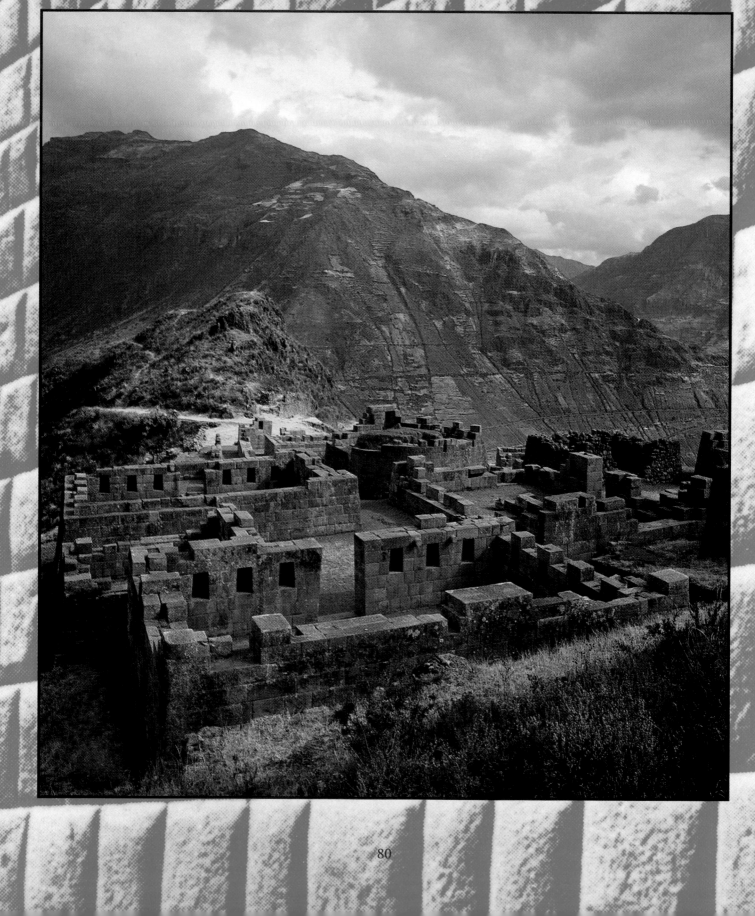

MAJESTIC PALACES FOR THE MOVABLE COURT

During the heyday of the Inca empire, its supreme rulers built several opulent estates in the countryside around Cuzco. Accompanied by his retinue of courtiers, an emperor could retire to one of his pastoral retreats and conduct state business away from the hustle and bustle of the capital.

The great ruler Pachacuti was responsible for some of the finest of these country residences. He chose locales that appealed to him for their scenic beauty and then, by royal fiat, mobilized the empire's unlimited labor force to realize the projects. Pachacuti's private estates remained in the hands of his descendants for generations after his death.

But these sites were more than just a home away from home for the godlike Inca leader; the surrounding acreage was terraced and put under cultivation with miles of irrigation canals to augment his worldly wealth.

Such was the efficiency of Inca agricultural methods that food production from these lands not only supplied the needs of the permanent staff and the visiting bureaucracy but also generated a surplus, which, under the strict tenets of Inca hierarchy, became the personal property of the ruler himself.

Pachacuti's lodge stood on the site of this spring at Tambo Machay. Channels carved into the polygonal retaining walls created fountains for the sacred waters. The niches in the upper wall possibly once held religious idols, testifying to the spring's spiritual significance.

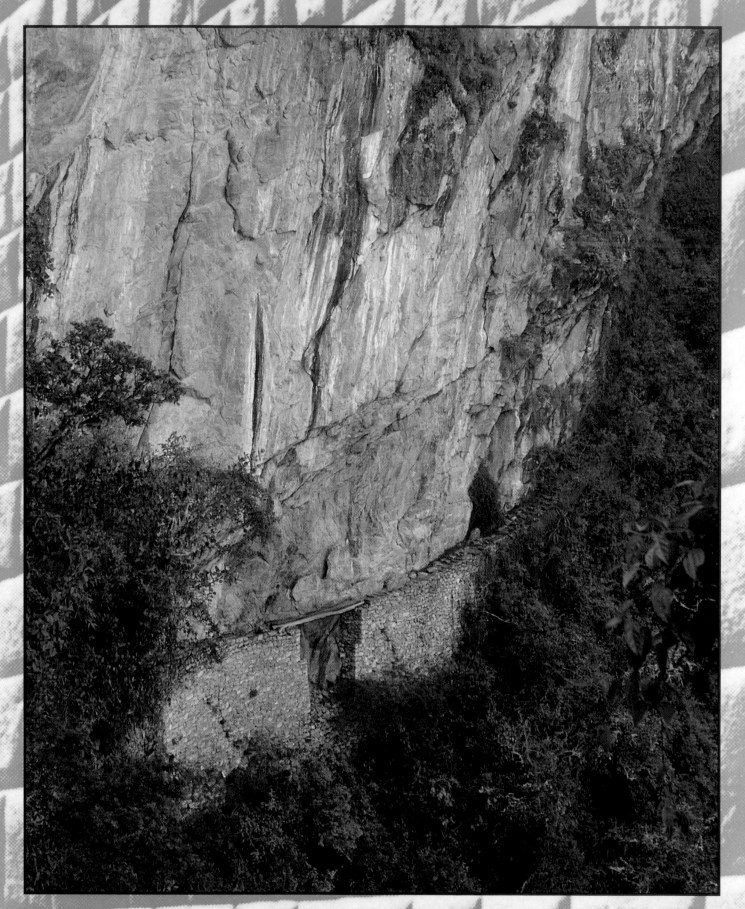

Hugging the sheer face of a cliff, the dizzying road to Machu Picchu typifies the
Incas' mastery of engineering techniques.
The trail was deliberately laid along this
vertiginous route for defensive reasons;
where logs now span the chasm at center,
a drawbridge once served as a strategi-
cally placed checkpoint.

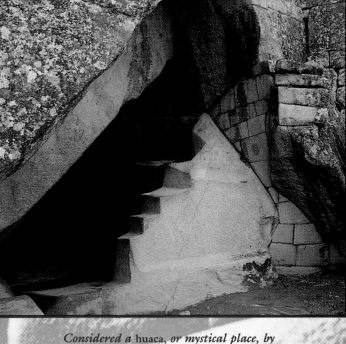

Considered a huaca, *or mystical place, by the Incas, this natural fissure sits beneath the so-called Temple of the Sun at Machu Picchu. Stonemasons carved steps, altars, and niches into its granite interior and constructed a wall, at right, to link it to the temple above.*

REVERENCE FOR THE LIVING ROCK

The Incas regarded stone not only as a strong and abundant building material, but also with undisguised spiritual devotion. In the barren highlands that spawned Inca theology, stone is omnipresent. The stark pinnacles of the surrounding Andes formed the axis of the Incas' known universe, and rocky outcrops punctuated the landscape throughout their realm. Many of these geological features were deemed *huacas*—mystical places that possessed inherent powers of their own.

It is no wonder, then, that the unsurpassed skills of the Inca stonemasons were applied to natural rock formations—for both utilitarian and religious purposes.

Using the same type of stone tools and techniques with which Protzen experimented on freestanding building blocks, these long-vanished, anonymous craftsmen created monuments to their culture that have survived Spanish depredation, massive earthquakes, and half a millennium of wind and rain.

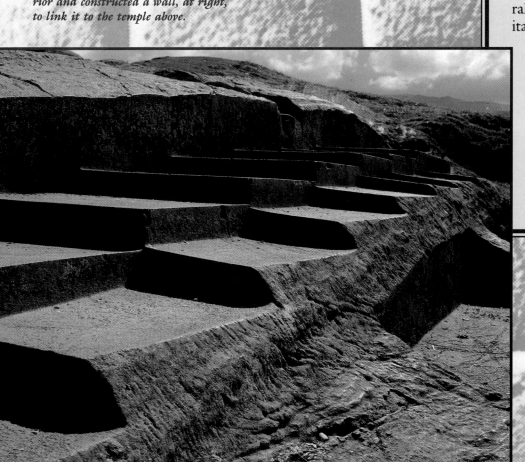

Broad ledges cut into a rocky hilltop overlooking the fortresslike temple of Sacsahuaman were once referred to as the Throne of the Inca. Current scientific opinion, however, holds that the site had a spiritual function and was probably used for either the placement of sacrifices or the performance of religious rituals.

BORROWERS OF GREATNESS

Mighty empire builders though they may have been, the Incas were not quite all that they seemed to the conquering Spaniards, who confessed such amazement over their achievements. What the Spaniards did not know is that the Incas had been quick to appropriate the technology of others. Virtually all the marvels of their civilization—from the great stone structures at Cuzco, to the agricultural terraces of the mountain slopes, to the 15,000 miles of paved highways that knitted the empire together—took their inspiration from earlier ethnic groups. Even the magnificent gold artifacts that so enchanted the Spaniards were largely the work of other hands.

Not that the Incas gave much credit. As their court historians told it, little of consequence had occurred in the Andes before the Incas' rise to power. Whatever culture the region enjoyed, they implied, had originated with the Incas. The truth is that civilized life in the Andes went back at least 3,000 years. Archaeologists have found temples in the highlands and great cities in the coastal deserts that were as remote in time from the age of Inca greatness as is the Athens of Pericles from the Athens of modern Greece. But if the Incas were inheritors, they were able to mark the accomplishments of those who preceded them with the stamp of their own genius.

From the beginning, life in the areas that would become the

These hammered-gold gauntlets probably sheathed the hands of a noble Chimu mummy. The designs—warriors in battle dress and geometric patterns—reflect the Chimu practice of tattooing their bodies.

Inca empire posed unique challenges to the Indians who inhabited them. In valleys leading to the coastal desert, for example, the climate was so dry that no more than an inch or two of rain fell in any single year. While some groups made their living along the coast as fishermen, harvesting the rich protein bounty churned up by the colder temperatures of the currents sweeping north from Antarctica, others in the valleys tended garden plots of squash and beans, and eventually corn, on small green patches made possible by water from rivers gushing from the heights. Settlement spread as people began moving inland, there to meet other challenges posed by the extremes of weather and altitude. Towns grew up around ceremonial centers, then turned into cities filled with all the creative bustle of civilized Stone Age life. As long ago as 2500 BC (and perhaps before), early Peruvians, working in adobe brick, built temple pyramids in various coastal areas of Peru that rival Egypt's in their monumental scale. A spectacular example of these, carbon-dated to 1800-1500 BC, stands 10 stories tall at a site called Pampa de las Llamas-Moxeke.

One of the first students of Andean culture to explore this ancient progression was the German archaeologist Max Uhle. As early as the 1890s, Uhle commenced digging at various burial sites in the mountains and along the Pacific coast, unearthing pottery and textiles and comparing their decorative motifs. His findings enabled him to sketch out a relative chronology of ancient Peruvian styles.

A site that fascinated Uhle was Tiahuanaco, known for its ancient and mysterious set of megalithic monuments near the shores of Lake Titicaca in present-day Bolivia. Titicaca, at 12,500 feet above the Pacific, is the world's highest body of navigable water, and one of the most remote. The surrounding puna, or treeless tableland, is bleak beyond imagining—a plateau of rock and hardy ichu grass, swept by bitter high-country winds, and stretching to a fringe of distant mountain ranges. The region is said to have four seasons per day: Spring when the sun rises, summer at noon, autumn in the evening, and winter as the frigid mountain darkness settles in.

But the ruins that stand near Lake Titicaca are astonishing. Uhle made drawings and ground plans of what were probably three limestone temples and four administrative structures, set on a series of raised platforms and in sunken rectangular courts. Like all visitors who come here, he marveled at the edifices' monolithic stonework.

First detected in 1931, this rampart cuts across the Andean foothills through the southern portion of the Kingdom of Chimor. What had looked like disjointed piles of rock and adobe from the ground emerged as a linear barrier 50 miles long when finally viewed from the air.

Some of the blocks are as big as small rooms and weigh up to 100 tons. They were cut and fitted with such precision that mortar was not used, nor even necessary. Already in ruins by the time the Incas took over the region in the 15th century, a legend arose that Tiahuanaco had been erected at the dawn of time, by a race of gods or giants.

Little is known about the Tiahuanacans and their culture. But archaeology, using carbon dating, has provided a specific time frame for their monuments. The Tiahuanaco temple complex began taking shape, it seems, around the first century AD, then expanded 500 years later and continued to grow for another five centuries. Among the legacies of this mysterious culture is a massive doorway, the Gate of the Sun, hewn from a single block of stone. Carved on its lintel is the figure of a god with round, staring eyes, and a halo of serpent and feline heads. In each hand is a staff, one tipped with a condor head. The god's image appears not only at Tiahuanaco, but throughout the Peruvian Andes. Uhle, excavating at Pachacamac, a shrine on the coast near Lima that had been revered from ancient times through the Inca period, found an abundance of Tiahuanacan motifs. In coastal ruins to the north, close to the city of Trujillo, he uncovered further images of the deity. Clearly, Tiahuanaco had spread its influence across much of the territory later occupied by the Incas.

To the north of Tiahuanaco lay the empire of the Huari, so named after the ruins of their capital city. This highland polity dominated the very region where the Incas would come to power. The Huari flourished during the same period as the Tiahuanacans, and they too had disappeared as a political force by Inca times. Their physical legacy consisted of the fieldstone walls of their well-planned cities and bureaucratic posts and the network of interconnecting roadways between them.

Before its disappearance, the Huari empire stretched north from the valley of Cuzco nearly to the border of present-day Ecuador, and from the central cordillera down to the coast. Its influence is recognizable in the urban planning of the Chimu, a dynasty arising around the ninth century AD. When Topa Inca Yupanqui, the 10th ruler of the Incas, conquered the Kingdom of Chimor between 1465 and 1470, he took over a culture that in some respects was considerably more advanced than his own. The adobe-brick capital of Chan Chan was one of the largest cities in South America, with a population of perhaps 36,000 people. Chimu croplands, in the river valleys bordering the coastal deserts, were watered by an irrigation system of unequaled scope and efficiency. Chimu craftsmen were among the best in America; much of the Inca gold that later bedazzled the conquistadors was wrought by Chimu hands. Confronted by such displays of wealth and talent, the Incas did the wise thing—they absorbed the Chimu culture, getting their artisans to work for them and thus becoming, in a way, the disciples of their own vassals.

When the great Pachacuti came to power, he had the opportunity to see firsthand achievements of the other Andean cultures, past and present, as he marched from conquest to conquest. Like the Spaniards, he could only have been impressed, and it is possible that he found himself wishing not only to duplicate some of their accomplishments but also to surpass their collective imperial grandeur. Early on he launched the rebuilding of Cuzco. The city apparently had developed as a haphazard cluster of modest fieldstone dwellings, many of them one-room structures. Pachacuti swept these away, then laid out a roughly rectangular street plan, replacing the earlier structures with palaces and temples, including the bastionlike Sacsahuaman temple. For his model, he looked to the civic monuments of two earlier cultures: the temples at Tiahuanaco, and the great walled compounds of the Huari.

The lords of Huari were in some respects the Incas' closest cultural ancestors. Both were highlanders, both conquerors; and like the Incas, they seem to have kept their subjects on a fairly tight rein, sending out orders and accepting tribute along miles of well-tended roadways. Above all, the Huari were consummate builders—the first true urban planners in South America. They laid out one of their administrative centers, Pikillacta, only 17 miles southeast of Cuzco, with the foursquare precision of a military encampment, with more than 700 buildings of monumental stature, many as large as three stories high and 150 feet long. The walls of these structures consisted of fieldstone set in mud cement smoothed over with coats of clay and gypsum plaster; from

Modern Peruvian archaeology began with the German Max Uhle (right), *the first scholar to document a long succession of Andean cultures that predated the Incas. One of the sites he investigated was Tiahuanaco* (below), *the ceremonial center of a civilization that flourished in the first millennium AD. Through Uhle's efforts, much information about the achievements of this prodigious and enigmatic people, long the subject of fanciful legends, has come to light.*

the evidence of surviving ruins, some measured 6 feet thick and rose up nearly 50 feet from their foundations. A system of underground conduits provided drainage for the complex.

Several archaeologists believe that Pachacuti took his general city plan from Pikillacta. He seems to have lifted directly both the street grid and the basic layout of the *cancha,* an enclosed dwelling area with an interior courtyard that became standard for dwellings in the Inca imperial style. But Cuzco's true glory lay not in its mimicry of Huari order but in the perfectly crafted cut-stone blocks that formed its finest buildings. And for these the inspiration was drawn from the monuments of Tiahuanaco.

Like its Tiahuanaco counterpart, Inca stonework is massive and finely hewn. The Incas cut some blocks jigsaw fashion; one famous stone in the wall of the Hatun Rumiyoc, the palace of the sixth ruler, Inca Roca, displays no fewer than 12 corners on its outer face, all interlocking perfectly with the adjoining stones. For other walls, they finished stones of uniform size and laid them in even rows like brickwork. To ensure that such stones would fit and hold, they made the top of each slightly concave, forming a saucerlike depression that would cradle the stone above, which bulged out on its bottom surface. By keying or locking stones together at the point of greatest strain they created walls that could withstand earthquakes; the tremors might lift the stones briefly, but the stones would just as quickly settle down into position. Even more astonishing is how the Incas managed to cut the gigantic blocks seen in their surviving structures in Cuzco and elsewhere. "They are as big as forest tree trunks," wrote Pizarro's secretary, Pedro Sancho, of the huge foundation stones of the Sacsahuaman fortified temple. "Three carts could not carry even the smallest of them." He did not exaggerate—one of the stones is estimated to weigh 86 tons, another 126 tons, and one is so large that if it were hollow, three carts could fit inside it. Another chronicler,

The coastal road—part of a system that encompassed at least 15,000 miles of paved highway—crosses Chile's Atacama Desert with a minimum of deviations. The Spanish were astounded at the Incas' ability to transmit orders and communiqués across their vast holdings. Chasqui runners, or royal couriers, linked the four corners of the empire by running short relays at top speed, moving messages—and sometimes delicacies such as fresh fish for the emperor's table—as many as 250 miles a day. The size and complexity of this network is depicted on the map at right; the main north-south highway alone stretched 3,600 miles.

verts ensuring proper drainage. Elsewhere, surfaces might be plastered with a tough, weatherproof compound of corn leaves, pebbles, and clay. Along the hardpan of the coast the road was left unpaved; but stone pillars marked the shoulders, and along some stretches low walls of stone or adobe were built to keep out the sand and to prevent the llama caravans or relay messengers from straying. On the main routes, boundary stones marked the distances.

Road widths varied with the terrain, from nearly 20 feet in the flats, along the desert and puna, down to 3 feet in the mountain passes. Wherever possible, the roads were laid out with linear precision. The Inca engineers seemed to prefer to surmount obstacles rather than evade them. And since the highways were used only by pedestrians or surefooted llamas, there was virtually no limit on the steepness of the gradient. This made for rugged travel in the highlands, involving switchbacks, dizzying flights of stairs, and even ladders cut into bedrock. On the route between Machu Picchu and Vilcabamba, where the path hugs the side of a mountain escarpment, a 12-foot-high man-made stone embankment carries the roadway. At another place, the road passes through a tunnel-like rock cut, 15 feet long, made by enlarging a natural fissure. The sloping tunnel is tall enough for a man to walk through and has low steps cut into its floor.

The road builders faced their toughest challenge, however, when spanning the region's numerous waterways. Although many rivers were fordable, some were so swift that crossing was difficult even where the water was only knee-deep. Narrow rivers or small streams on level ground could be bridged with logs or with corbeled stone archways. Wide, slow-moving rivers called for a different approach—pontoon bridges made from highly buoyant reed boats, tethered together and covered by a wooden roadbed. When it came to spanning the deep river gorges of the montaña, the road builders often rigged an *oroya,* a kind of cable car that hung from a heavy rope of twisted vines or ichu grass strung from one bank to the other. The passenger, crouching in a reed basket that dangled from the cable, would be pulled across by men on the far side. But sometimes there was no basket, and Father Cobo tells what happened then: "They just tie the man securely so that if he becomes alarmed and faints, he cannot fall, and hanging in the air from the cable by a large wooden hook, he is pulled from one side to the other."

Taking the most direct route up and over the region's innumerable mountains, Inca roadways included dizzying stairways and cliff-face paths cut into living rock. Chasqui runners and hardy llamas were undaunted by the heart-stopping gradients, but Spanish conquistadors found them a formidable barrier to the safe and swift passage of their cavalry.

While this makeshift basket arrangement worked fine for individual travelers on secondary roads, major highways demanded something more substantial. To carry people and cargo across the mountain torrents, the Incas built suspension bridges. These rank among the outstanding triumphs of their engineering. A pair of stone pylons was raised on either bank to anchor a set of massive cables woven of ichu grass, each "thick as the body of a boy," according to Cobo. Two cables functioned as guardrails; three others supported the roadbed, made of plaited branches. The bridges sagged from their own weight, and they swayed alarmingly in the wind. But they were strong enough to support nobles carried in their litters and, later, the Spaniards with their horses. To ensure safety, the cables were replaced at least once a year by local villagers whose only task was to keep them in repair. The most spectacular of the bridges, slung over the Apurimac canyon on the main road north from Cuzco, reached 220 feet from bank to bank, while the river churned 118 feet below.

For all the high drama attendant upon using the Inca highways, their builders strove to make travel swift and pleasant. Along some stretches they planted fruit trees watered by means of irrigation ditches; travelers could pick the fruit for refreshment. The builders erected tambos (roadside shelters) at intervals of 15 to 30 miles, and provided corrals for llamas. At each, a local caretaker kept stocks of provisions—corn, lima beans, dried potatoes, dried meat. Recent archaeological investigations reveal that the Incas constructed and maintained tambos on every road throughout the empire, totaling around 1,000 in all. Colonial records report an attempt by the Spaniards to keep the tambos going as an integral part of the highway network, but with far less success than the Incas had had.

These way stations, like the qollqas, illustrate the importance of storage to the smooth running of the Inca empire. But they would have been of little use had the Incas not created an effective agricultural economy. To take care of the food needs of the burgeoning empire, they had to reshape entire landscapes—and they did so by terracing mountainsides, straightening rivers, filling or draining marshes, and channeling water into the deserts to make them bloom. In a realm that was mostly vertical and whose horizontal stretches tended to be either arid steppe or outright desert, few areas lent themselves readily to farming.

Agricultural terraces can be seen throughout the empire—

Made of 22,000 feet of hand-braided ichu grass, this authentic modern reconstruction of an Inca suspension bridge is anchored to the original stone abutments on either side of the gorge. These graceful spans represented the pinnacle of Inca highway engineering. Local peasants performed continual maintenance on the structures as part of their mit'a, *or obligation to public service.*

tion possible despite the 12,500-foot altitude. But even with this advantage, if the local inhabitants had not resorted to the raised-field method of growing crops, their output would have been limited.

The raised fields were created by digging out parallel channels and heaping up the soil thereby removed in rectangular platforms, 12 to 30 feet wide, 30 to 300 feet long, and 3 feet high. The American geographer William Denevan, one of the first to study the raised fields, estimates that the entire Titicaca project would have required 145 million working days to construct. The efficiency of the design, however, made the work both desirable and necessary. The dredged-up earth was exceedingly fertile, and the platforms' elevation improved drainage and minimized the effects of flooding. The channels did much more than provide moisture during times of drought; they acted as heat sinks, absorbing the warmth of the sun during the day and releasing it at night when the air temperature plunged. An in-

GOLD AND SILVER: "SWEAT OF THE SUN, TEARS OF THE MOON"

No other peoples in all of pre-Columbian America had a greater repertoire of metallurgic techniques than the Chimu and the Incas. Indeed, in many ways the Peruvian craftsmen of that period were more sophisticated than their contemporaries in the Old World, even if their tools were not.

Using smooth, hard stones as both hammer and anvil, the metalsmiths pounded out the basic shape of the object from raw ingots. They then added their distinctive artistic touches by hammering the piece against a bas-relief template or etching it freehand with a stylus.

Although artisans sometimes employed closed- and open-mold casting, cold-hammering was the most common practice. To prevent the metal from becoming brittle as it was worked, it was sometimes subjected to a process called annealing, which means it was heated repeatedly to free it from internal stress and maintain pliability.

Graceful, wavelike motifs outline the border of this golden tumi, *or ceremonial knife, incised by a Chimu artisan who worked without benefit of steel engraving tools. Scholars are uncertain as to what the panel of anthropomorphic figures represents.*

sulating blanket was thus formed that helped both to keep the plants from freezing and to extend the growing season.

In a dramatic example of what is referred to today as experimental archaeology, which is a way of learning about the past by re-creating aspects of it to study, a team of agronomists and archaeologists led by Dr. Clark Erickson of the University of Pennsylvania duplicated the prehistoric raised beds and grew two of the crops that an analysis of ancient pollen recovered at the sites indicated might

This spectacular funerary mask of hammered, painted gold was created just to be buried with its owner. Almond-shaped eyes and rounded earplugs—worn by nobility—are common features of the art of the Kingdom of Chimor.

Silver objects (left) illustrate Chimu mastery of different metalworking techniques. The pieces were hammered, then soldered together. The musician fingers his panpipe with tattooed hands. The deer—an important food source—served as a burial offering.

107

have been cultivated 1,000 to 3,000 years ago—potatoes and quinoa. At harvest time, the yields from the raised beds surpassed everyone's wildest expectations. The normal potato crop in the region is 8 tons per acre. The first season, the return was more than double that. The following year, 1984, production reached 30 tons an acre.

With success like this, why were the fields abandoned? One theory proposed by Dr. Erickson suggests that the Titicaca area became depopulated as a result of disruption caused by the Inca conquest. Furthermore, by that time, the Incas were able to produce more than enough food for their expanding empire by using their improved terracing and irrigation methods, which often enabled them to harvest two crops a year.

The practicality and ingenuity of the Incas extended to all that they did, including metalworking, an old craft they raised to new heights. In 1928, some children playing near their small Peruvian

A bronze ceremonial tumi, *with its characteristic half-moon-shaped blade, tapers at the handle into the elongated neck of a llama. The motif is appropriate, since llamas were often ritualistically sacrificed and their entrails analyzed by priests to divine the future.*

Andean men had very sparse facial hair. Shaving was unnecessary; any whiskers were simply plucked. Silver tweezers (above)—*and sometimes gold—did the job for the elite; the humbler bronze sufficed for the lower classes. Father Bernabé Cobo likened the Incas' wispy beards to "a handful of horsehair" and noted their amazement at the sight of the hirsute Spanish.*

village discovered a grave containing gold objects more than 2,000 years old. By the height of the Chimu dynasty in the 15th century, though, goldsmithing had developed from an individual pursuit to a highly organized and controlled personal industry serving the nobility. At the time of the Inca conquest of Chimor, the Chimu were acknowledged to be the Andes' most accomplished metalworkers.

The Chimu smiths and their Inca counterparts drew upon a wider repertoire of goldworking techniques than did any other Americans of their day. They cut pectorals and earplugs from hammered gold sheets, shaped cups and dishes around wooden templates, cast beads and statues, used gilding and plating, and closed loose edges with a type of soldering. They were adept at inlay, repoussé, and filigree. And as with all else they did, they managed to create masterpieces without, as Father Cobo said, "tongs, hammers, files, chisels, burins as well as the other implements used by our

For the Incas and many Andean peoples, gold symbolized the sun, and seldom more graphically than in this shimmering pectoral six inches in diameter. Sheets of gold were hammered out, then pierced and threaded so they could be hung around the neck as a pendant.

Since all gold belonged to the emperor, the Incas saw no need to conceal it. Only burial offerings such as this elegant jug, beaker, and vase escaped the Spaniards' systematic campaign to loot the empire of all its treasures.

silversmiths." Another Spaniard, the historian Juan de Torquemada, wrote in 1613 that the smiths wrought objects of a beauty "greatly surpassing that of our Spanish jewelers because they could make birds whose heads, tongues, and wings could be made to move, and animals in whose paws they placed trinkets that seemed to dance."

Unlike silver, gold was, for the most part, not actually mined but rather panned or gathered in nugget or dust form. But where mines did exist, the labor required to extract ore was not deemed particularly onerous. Unlike later mines run by the Spaniards, whose relentless demands led to the death of many conscripted workers, the Inca operations were apparently models of enlightened management. The workday lasted from noon to sunset to prevent exhaustion in the oxygen-deprived air of the high altitudes; wives—who were allowed to stay with their husbands while they paid off their labor tax—cooked for their men, holidays were frequent, and each worker could return to his home after working his turn.

Bellows and blast furnaces were unknown; smelting temperatures of more than 1,000 degrees centigrade were reached in terra-cotta wind furnaces called *huairas*. In areas where a lack of wind prevented this type of furnace from being built, the workers, noted Garcilaso, "blasted by means of tubes of copper, the length of half a cubit, more or less, according as the furnace was large or small. The tubes were closed at one end, leaving one small hole through which the air could rush with more force. As many as 8, 10, or 12 of these were put together, and they went round the fire blowing with the tubes." The Incas' methods may have been rudimentary, but their output was extraordinary, and even those Spaniards whose task was to melt down the silver and gold objects looted from the empire must have felt some qualms about doing so. Not all production was artistic in nature; the Incas also manufactured practical items from tin, silver, copper, and lead, and from alloys of two or more metals.

As sophisticated and worldly-wise as the Europeans considered themselves to be, they were never able to adapt and adjust and operate productively in the harsh environment of Peru to the degree that the Incas and their predecessors had. After the conquest, the silver and gold began to run out, the terraces and irrigation canals were abandoned, the bridges were allowed to rot away, and the surviving buildings were neglected and left to decay. The legacy of the Incas, however, would live on in the spirit of their accomplishments and in their indomitable will in the face of adversity.

A t the peak of its gilded glory in the 14th and 15th centuries, the Kingdom of Chimor spread 600 miles along the Peruvian coast. The Chimu, whose civilization reached full flower just prior to the ascendancy of the Incas, had reason to be proud of themselves. They were warriors who subdued all their potential rivals. They were city builders whose seaside capital of Chan Chan was most likely the biggest metropolis in pre-Columbian South America. They were farmers and engineers who built a large and ingenious network of canals to convey water from Andean streams to their parched and rainless homeland.

But most of all the Chimu were superb artisans who created objects of extraordinary intricacy and beauty from gold and silver; wood, shells, and bones; and feathers, cotton, and wool. Indeed, so numerous were the metalsmiths, carvers, weavers, and engravers of Chan Chan that archaeologists believe that out of an estimated population of 36,000 as many as 12,000 devoted themselves to arts production.

When archaeologists excavating the ruins of Chan Chan shifted their focus in the 1970s from the walled palaces of the Chimu kings to the barrios of the proletariat, they marveled at the craft remains they found in small houses and cramped workshops—ingots, hammers, bins stocked with cotton, unfinished textiles. The fact that so much of value had been left in the ruins suggested a hasty exit, probably at the time of the Inca conquest of the Chimu between 1465 and 1470. But where did the artisans go? The Incas knew a good thing when they saw it and brought the most talented of Chan Chan's citizens to their capital of Cuzco. Doubtless it was the hands of gifted Chimu designers, ironically, that produced many of the golden treasures that so dazzled and excited the conquistadors—and thus hastened the end of the Incas themselves.

THE GOLDEN CITY OF THE DEAD

The Chimu capital of Chan Chan resembled no place else. Where other cities had plazas and boulevards, Chan Chan's core was a succession of royal compounds archaeologists call *ciudadelas* (little cities) that lay concealed behind adobe walls up to 30 feet high and 2,000 feet long. Each consisted of a maze of corridors connecting storerooms, officelike chambers, courtyards, residential quarters, and burial mounds.

Archaeologists at first thought that the ciudadelas segregated the population socially or occupationally, but later research seems to indicate that each compound was in fact a palace. When a king died, he was probably laid to rest in his own abode, beside an ample selection of worldly goods and dozens, perhaps hundreds, of young female sacrificial victims. The property, in turn, passed to his relations, while his successor took up residence in a new compound.

Smaller compounds adjoining the ciudadelas, probably the homes of nobles and high-ranking bureaucrats, formed a buffer between the royal palaces and the barrio dwellings of the commoners. The society that emerges from the archaeological record was urban, well organized, materialistic, theocratic (kings were thought to be divine), and aggressive. But its strange, inward-looking capital, with its walls-within-walls palaces that ultimately became royal mausoleums, was also, even in its own time, a city of the dead.

Chan Chan's urban sprawl is evident in this photograph of a portion of its 10-square-mile expanse and in the schematic map (below) of the city's core area. The map shows locations of the walled ciudadelas, or royal compounds (gold), *the barrios, or artisans' quarters* (brown), *and sunken gardens* (light gold), *and also identifies important structures within the compound seen in the foreground of the photograph. The sprawling ciudadelas occupied about a quarter of Chan Chan. Large gardens, like the greenish rectangle in the picture, were placed below ground level so that plants could draw directly on the water table. Regrettably for the Chimu, the plots did not produce enough food for the citizenry. More crops were planted in outlying fields irrigated by canals. The Incas conquered the Chimu by cutting off Chan Chan's water supply.*

1 Burial mound
2 Sunken garden
3 Ceremonial plazas
4 Audiencias, or reception areas
5 Large storage area for prestige goods

HUMBLE MUD TRANSFORMED INTO HIGH ART

Art was everywhere in Chimor—on clothing and jewelry, on knives and litters and household utensils, and most of all on the walls. Elaborate, often geometrical friezes covered walls at the great Chan Chan palaces. In a city of straight lines and right angles the Chimu filled the vast adobe surfaces around them with friezes fashioned three different ways—by carving directly in the wet clay, by pressing the clay into large forms,

and by molding the material in relief planes in a technique similar to embossing. Although everything in Chan Chan today is pale ocher like the surrounding earth, the friezes, most of which had maritime themes, were originally plastered and in some cases brightly painted. Surviving designs are symmetrical and stylized, often interspersing a geometric pattern with depictions of mammals, birds, fish, and mythical creatures. They look like textile patterns transposed to adobe, which they might well have been.

Though recognizing the Chimu as master architects, archaeologists wondered why Chan Chan's walls were built in sections that had no structural or artistic rationale. One expert, combining the wall segments with the Chimu policy of labor as taxation, theorizes that a single unit of adobe wall represented the production of one work crew in a given time period. However they were made, Chan Chan's mud walls were built to last. Generally about 13 feet wide at the base and tapering to 4 to 5 feet at the top, they have withstood 600 to 800 years of sporadic earthquakes without disappearing.

The restored friezes on the Huaca del Dragon (above), a sacred site outside Chan Chan, portray arched, double-headed serpents and other mythical as well as real creatures. The design at the near end shows a clash of mythic figures surrounded by masked men bearing spears. The structure was probably dedicated to the moon goddess, Si, who, rather than the sun god, was worshiped as the supreme deity by the Chimu because of her power over the sea, storms, and crops.

These bas-relief friezes in the Ciudadela Velarde have sea themes. The first depicts a small reed boat called a caballito (little horse) that has persisted in the area to the present day. On the boat's prow sits a cormorant. The second frieze incorporates fish, squid, and other marine life still to be found in local waters.

Diamond-shaped carvings line the wall of this now roofless audiencia, or receiving room, in a Chan Chan palace. The niches and bins are thought to be either for the display of precious objects or for storage. The walls' rounded edges are the result of centuries of weathering.

AN OYSTER AS REVERED AS GOLD

An old legend tells of the first king of a province north of Chan Chan eventually conquered by the Chimu. The story goes that he arrived by sea, bringing with him wives, concubines, attendants, and eight deputies, one of whom was charged with scattering before him a carpet of red dust produced from spiny oyster shells. The species *(below)*, called *spondylus*, was held in high esteem in Chimor. Archaeologists found the reddish shells of the mollusk—whole, in pieces, and crushed to powder—at every royal burial site. One cache of *spondylus* was discovered interred alone, as if the shells themselves were royalty. But the most remarkable fact about this mollusk is that it is native not to Peruvian waters but to the warmer seas off Ecuador.

The question of why the *spondylus* was so prized remains a riddle. One scholar speculates that its importance is linked with El Niño storms that periodically bring catastrophic floods to the Peruvian coast. By this theory the oysters move south in the warm El Niño currents that kill most of the indigenous cold-water fish. They were thus an omen of death—and, perhaps, a totem to be venerated.

The intricate neckpiece above, which may have been worn by a Chimu king, combines vivid spondylus *and mussel shells with jet and a mother-of-pearl fringe. Despite its numerous beads, it was made without a fabric backing, and is held together instead with cotton thread.*

Spiny outside, shells of the mollusk spondylus *reveal their colorful interior. When Pizarro's men captured a balsa raft in their first contact with the Incas, they found shells like these in its cargo.*

116

In a society without wheeled vehicles, the wondrously decorated wooden litter below found near Chan Chan was the equivalent of a royal limousine. The gold, turquoise, shells, and wooden carvings artfully added to the back of the litter, seen here, depict masked and bewigged figures representing a dignitary flanked by two attendants in an audiencia.

The spondylus-and-stone mosaic inlaid on the wooden bowl (above) illustrates how the shells were gathered. The detail work shows a boat with a cabin, the divers below, boatmen holding their lifelines, and depictions of the shell itself.

Made from the feathers of a blue-and-yellow macaw like the one at left, this tunic features a pattern of lordly pelicans borne on litters by lesser birds. Chimu featherworkers were partial to two other species of macaws—the scarlet and the red-and-green—along with Muscovy ducks and paradise tanagers.

RESPLENDENT RAIMENT FOR THE CHOSEN FEW

These wood-and-feather earplugs blend the finely chopped plumes of macaws (red and yellow), parrots (green), and tanagers or honeycreepers (purple). The wooden figures have been carved so that they are raised from the surface as in relief.

Chimu workshops were team enterprises. Archaeologists sifting through the dust of 600-year-old barrios frequently found implements for metalsmithing in the same small rooms with spindles and woodworking tools, suggesting a division of labor that doubtless would have facilitated the creation of items like clothing adorned with feathers and gold, or wooden pieces inlaid with stones and shells.

While the everyday outfit for men was a tunic and loincloth, and for women a horizontally wrapped dress, on ceremonial occasions the Chan Chan nobles turned out in brilliantly colored feathers or in garments of luxurious alpaca and vicuna wool. Since wool came from the highlands, and feathers from the macaws, parrots, and other birds of the Amazon basin, obtaining them demanded a far-reaching trade network. The wool arrived at the manufacturing nexus at Chan Chan already spun and dyed; there it was woven into richly patterned cloth.

Curiously, Chimu textile goods were found to be more widely dispersed in Peru after the Inca conquest of Chimor than before. The most likely explanation: The Incas collected textiles as taxes and then recirculated them as rewards or payment.

The tassels and tapestry weave on this tunic are probably dyed alpaca wool. Since wool had to be imported, it was used sparingly, often in tapestry bands or as embroidery on cotton. The design here is the familiar Chimu motif of two men in a boat. The slits on the fringe were not cut but woven in; many Andean peoples deemed cutting fabric a sacrilege.

GLITTERING GARB THAT PROCLAIMED KINSHIP

For centuries, Andean peoples had been plucking gold from their streams and digging it out of their mountains. By Chimu times gold mining was a major industry; one account estimates that 6,000 men toiled in the royal mines. The ore was smelted in hillside "wind furnaces," where air blowing through apertures in chimneys raised the temperature of the fires; or by lung power, with miners blowing through tubes to fan the smelters' flames. Shipped to Chan Chan in ingots, the metal was pounded into sheets with small stone hammers and fashioned into implements, decorative pieces, and ornaments for glittering garments like those shown here, using a variety of sophisticated methods including welding and soldering.

The Chimu valued gold not as wealth—they had no coinage—but as a symbol of power and prestige. With them, as with the Incas, none but the elite could garb themselves in gold. The lords of Chimu drank from golden goblets, combed their hair with golden combs, and plucked their whiskers with golden tweezers. To the Chimu, it appears, gold was treasured more as an idea than as a fact, as an essence rather than as an object. For them, the glow of gold was a luster that shone from within, an expression of royal power.

Spangled with 18-carat gold platelets, this ceremonial robe dates from the conquest of Chimor by the Incas. It may have draped the shoulders of a Chimu king or been specially created for an Inca ruler. Small masks are sewn into the geometrically patterned central band with characteristic Chimu symmetry.

The gold pieces on this shirt depict shells, frogs, and human faces along with geometric shapes that may have held emblematic meaning. Apparently, property in Chimu society was regarded as a divine right reserved for the nobility. Theft of such a valuable shirt would thus have been seen as a crime both religious and civil, meriting the death of not only the culprit but also his parents and siblings.

The bag at right, with layers of quadrangular gold disks covering its cloth base, was probably a gilded fashion accessory for a Chimu noble. Similar bags were employed by the Incas for holding coca leaves, the mildly narcotic stimulant that members of the Chimu nobility, in keeping with their status, may have used.

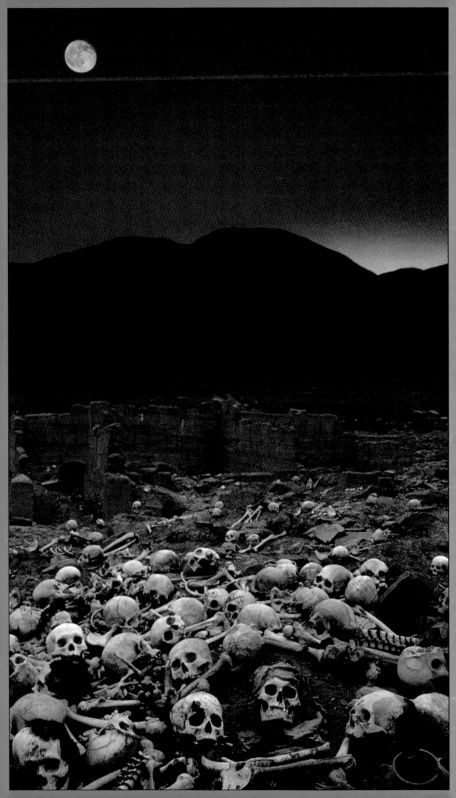

LIVES OF HARD WORK AND JOYOUS PLAY

When the Avenida Progreso, the coastal highway that wends east of Lima, Peru, was being constructed, laborers cut through a massive burial mound at the city's borders, exposing pre-Columbian graves and their contents—bits of pottery, wooden implements, mummy wrappings, bones, and skulls to which patches of dried skin and clumps of hair were still attached. To the inhabitants of Lima this would not have been regarded as a particularly unusual occurrence, since the grounds of many of their modern homes conceal such grim mementos and, as one observer wrote, "In cultivating their flower gardens, the residents are as likely to turn up skulls as stones."

Graveyards overflowing with ancient human remains abound between the Andes and the Pacific coast, from Ecuador to Chile, in the lands that once were provinces of the Inca empire. In the warm, dry coastal area, mummy bundles—bodies wound in yards of cloth—have been naturally preserved beneath the sands. Plundering the sites has provided a tidy income for generations of professional grave-robbers, known as *huaqueros*. Looking for relics, these thieves have greedily ravaged thousands of cemeteries, leaving behind fields of bones and desiccated bodies.

So it could hardly have seemed consequential to inhabitants of the modern city of Ancón, 20 miles north of Lima, when, in 1976,

Desecrated by hua-queros—local grave-robbers—for whatever valuables it contained, this pre-Inca cemetery near Lima bears mute witness to the once-glorious past—and to the damage inflicted on it by treasure hunters.

on the outskirts of their city, some unauthorized bulldozing blundered on mummified remains dating back to the century of Inca supremacy. It was merely the corpse of an unidentifiable woman, swathed in four layers of cloth wrappings together with her seemingly worthless possessions. The find might have been negligible, considering that during the past five decades, more than 2,000 mummy bundles had been uncovered in this region alone.

For Peruvian archaeologists, however, that casual discovery marked a valuable milestone in antiquarian research. The ransacking of ruins by huaqueros had contributed more than a million artifacts to the world's museums and private collections. But while producing abundant evidence of the diversity of the old culture, such scavenging had divorced the objects from their owners.

Now, however, archaeologists had access to a perfectly preserved mummy bundle, and they set about examining it with scientific care, meticulously unraveling it and photographing and recording each step of the process. Ultimately, the style of the bundle and of the numerous artifacts within it yielded a wealth of information about a woman of modest means who had lived some time between AD 1476 and 1532 *(pages 152-153)*.

The woman of Ancón—as she has come to be known—had been interred after long and laborious preparation and the donation of many gifts, and her burial reflected the high esteem accorded someone who had toiled with great industry and skill. This was the centuries-old way of Andean peoples—to find virtue and satisfaction in meaningful labor and to commemorate it in death. As Pedro Cieza de León reported immediately after the Spanish conquest: "No one who was lazy or tried to live by the work of others was tolerated; everyone had to work."

The Incas were quick to take advantage of this pervasive work ethic. Their imperial ambitions demanded that there be a class of citizens below the nobility, willing and able to wrest from the mountains and deserts the means to feed not only themselves but also a religious establishment that consumed enormous resources and an upper caste bent on creating a high culture. In the Andean peoples, the Incas had a vigorous peasantry that proved a worthy match for their requirements. In the details of their lives, these industrious folk revealed how creatively they had adapted to the hardships of their

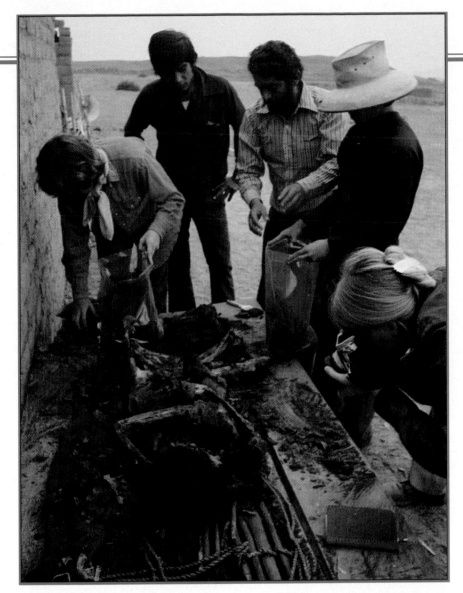

Dr. Karen Stothert (left) and a team from the National Institute of Culture in Lima assiduously photograph and catalog the contents of a mummy bundle they have just unwrapped. Scraps of cloth—here being gingerly placed in bags for later analysis—and the wood and rope pieces of a loom (bottom, center) buried with these remains of a wellborn but apparently not wealthy woman have provided archaeologists with much data on everyday life in the Inca empire.

varied environments, from the type of shoes they wore to the way they led their communal existence.

At the same time that they imposed a heavy work load on their subjects, the Incas—in seeming contradiction to their fundamental purpose—reduced the productivity of the peasants by devoting an inordinate amount of time and resources to great festivals, religious rituals, and public ceremonies. Approximately a third of the year was given over to these events. The largesse expended on them, however, was not lavished in vain; these celebrations forged links between the empire and the citizenry that made bearable the heavy demands of the Sapa Inca.

In this work-intensive society, laws rigidly regulated lives. They directed where people might live, what crops they might grow, how they might dress, even whom they might marry. An examination of these laws, as recorded by early Spanish chroniclers, as well as study of the surviving artifacts, has made it possible for scholars to reconstruct in minute detail the lifestyle of the common citizen of Tahuantinsuyu.

The dual sources of psychological support for the peasants in their daily round of endless tasks were the family and the *ayllu,* a patrilineal community consisting of a number of extended families living near one another and working collectively. There might be several ayllus in a large farm settlement, each occupying a block of dwellings surrounded by a walled-off area, each having its own revered ancestors, and each keeping to its designated section at festivals in the local village plaza.

The Incas superimposed on the ayllus their decimal-based bureaucratic organization of households into economic units of tens, hundreds, and thousands, each controlled by a curaca, the official who, among other duties, collected the taxes that the people paid in the form of agricultural produce and cloth. But for the ordinary family it was the ayllu that mattered, not the decimal unit to which the members happened to belong.

Every adult male within an ayllu, upon marriage, received from the Sapa Inca an allotment of land, or *topo,* that was just large enough to support himself and his wife. The size of the topo varied according to the fertility of the region, but if, for example, a topo measured two acres, then, according to the chronicler Garcilaso de la Vega, it was increased by a further two acres for each son the couple had to support, and by one-half acre for each daughter. As holder of a topo, the newly wed male was automatically registered as a *puric,* a tax-paying head of a household who was duly bound also to work on state lands and on property belonging to the religious establishment.

Modern scholars have pondered the role of the puric's wife in this setup. The ethnohistorian Irene Silverblatt has made much of the fact that the topo was allotted to a man only if he was married. She has suggested that although the land was formally presented to the husband, it was, in actuality, given to man and wife as a unit, indicating their complementary and thus equal share of the tax burden.

But who, in fact, worked harder? Some ethnohistorians have concluded that the plebeian wife, with small children, bore the brunt of the toil. Indeed, the Spanish conquistadors saw women as being virtually slaves of their husbands, condemned to a life of drudgery. It would be misleading, however, to judge the role of Andean women by the standards of the Spaniards, who equated hard physical labor with inferior status. Just as Father Bernabé Cobo saw these peasant women as "slaves," so the part-Andean chronicler, Felipe Huaman Poma de Ayala, whose mother was an Inca, viewed Spanish women as indolent and immoral because they remained idle even when they were able-bodied.

Within Andean culture, men and women regarded their working roles as mutually supportive and, for survival, necessarily so.

Within the ayllu, a sense of solidarity prevailed. The men got together to build the houses for newlyweds; and

Crafted by a skillful Chimu potter from the northern coastal region of the Incas' realm, this foot-long ceramic vessel depicts a fisherman with his lobster pot and catch. Images of traditional life are rare; Inca artisans generally eschewed realism and the human figure, concentrating instead on intricate geometric designs.

when one of them was called to serve out his mit'a, which might involve a stint in the army or on a public-works force, those who stayed behind took care of his topo on his family's behalf. At the time of the spring planting, when the ecclesiastical lands were plowed first, the men and women worked facing one another, chanting in time. The men turned up the soil with the *taclla,* a foot plow consisting of a pole about six feet long, with a footrest jutting out above its point of fire-hardened wood or bronze. The women followed behind, using a *lampa,* a simple hoe with a wide, chisel-shaped bronze blade, to break up the clods.

Nothing, of course, was more important to the ayllu than the success of each year's harvest. Throughout the empire the initial breaking of the soil was undertaken with great ceremony, the local dignitary making the first cut. The emperor and his court often participated on his own estates near Cuzco, where he used a gold-tipped taclla to initiate the planting. But Father Cobo observed that the Sapa Inca "soon stopped working, and after him the other officials and nobles stopped also, and sat down with the king to their banquets and festivals, which were especially notable on such days." After this symbolic gesture, and the festival that followed, the rest of the work would be left to the commoners. When they had finished preparing the property of the religious establishment, they would plow and sow the lands of the state, leaving their own allotments to be worked last of all.

Corn, the color of the sun, was by far the most valued crop and the food judged most fit for offering to the gods. But the peasants grew an enormous range of other plants—various beans and squashes, chili peppers, manioc, avocados, peanuts, gourds, cotton, coca, quinoa, a highland grain, and, not least of all, potatoes, of which there were more than 220 varieties. Such an assortment of food plants—some more suitable to one environment than another—involved planting and harvesting at different times of the year. As if caring for the fields was not enough, the peasants had to attend to myriad other tasks from fetching water, grinding corn, and brewing *chicha,* a beer usually made with a corn base, to weaving baskets and turning out earthenware jars used for cooking, serving, and storing

Doing double duty, a peasant woman nurses her baby while carrying a large aryballo, or chicha jug, strapped to her shoulders. The motif of this ceremonial vessel accurately illustrates the arduous lot of commoners in Peru's rugged, demanding environment; no respite from the usual workaday tasks was taken, not even by new mothers.

food. And in addition to all these chores, there was still the spinning and weaving of cloth to be done, for the family's needs and for the state.

While the Incas demanded that everyone work, they adjusted the rules to take into account the capacity or condition of the worker. The sick and the disabled were not required to support themselves. They were fed and clothed from the government storehouses, and only allotted duties suited to their physical condition. At the same time, however, the ever-pragmatic Inca regime ensured that the handicapped did not hold back any able-bodied citizen from gainful employment through their special needs. By law, a person with a major disability could only marry someone with a like disability—the blind to the blind, the deaf to the deaf, hunchbacks to hunchbacks, and dwarfs to dwarfs.

The elderly also received special consideration. A person was judged to have reached old age at around fifty. No longer qualified as fully able-bodied workers, those of advanced years were exempt from mit'a service and freed from taxation. No one was ever completely retired, however. For as long as possible the elderly were expected to undertake light duties, such as gathering brushwood, baby-sitting, preparing food and chicha, twisting ropes, and assisting at harvesttime.

Although women worked in the fields and cared for the children, they still were expected to weave. The woman of Ancón may have been a prodigious weaver; in any case, she was buried with a vast amount of cloth. There were about 17 yards of fabric in her wrappings alone, representing, by one scholarly estimate, more than 850 hours put in on spindle and loom. Two wicker workbaskets in her mummy bundle were packed with the implements and materials she had used. Women, including even noble Inca ladies, were forever spinning—as they walked and talked, as they kept an eye on their youngsters, as they watched over their cooking.

Men, too, were known to weave, although they more commonly took care of a family's apparel needs by cobbling sandals of untanned leather from the thick hide on the neck of the llama, tying their handiwork with woolen cords. Father Cobo describes a typical sandal as having a "sole which was shorter than the length of the foot, so that their toes extend out beyond the end of the sole, permitting them to grip with their toes when they are climbing uphill."

Farmers worked their land with tools like this wooden pitchfork and hoe. Men and women shared the planting, tending, and harvesting of crops on the family plot. In the rigid framework that regulated Inca agriculture, a part of each farmer's yield customarily reverted to the state.

In Inca society there was no opportunity to be lazy. Even childbearing women got little respite from the daily grind. The mother-to-be might be excused from agricultural work during the advanced stages of pregnancy, but otherwise she was expected to carry out all her household chores for as long as was physically possible. Not that the arrival of a child was trivialized. On the contrary, it was joyfully celebrated. From the Inca viewpoint, children were valued as future additions to the work force. Abortion, therefore—accomplished by beatings, fetal massages, and drugs—was, under the laws of the empire, a capital offense for both the mother and anyone who assisted her in the crime.

It was customary for the expectant mother to pray for safe delivery, and for the father to do his part to assure a successful outcome by fasting while she was in labor. But otherwise, childbirth was seen as a natural function to be conducted with a minimum of fuss. Although there were no midwives, mothers of twins were seen as having special expertise and sometimes assisted other mothers as they gave birth. More often, a peasant woman delivered her baby unaided, then bathed the newborn and herself in the nearest stream. Wherever she went, she would carry the infant bundled in a backpack tied across her chest with a shawl.

Every infant was breast-fed for as long as possible. Once the child had been weaned, its parents observed the ceremony called *rutuchicoy,* a feast attended by relations and friends. Here, the senior male relative would cut off a lock of the youngster's hair. Other guests followed suit, and each presented the child with a gift, usually cloth-

In this drawing, a woman at the time of the Incas harvests potatoes with a hoe similar to the example shown on the opposite page, while a man turns the soil with a taclla, or foot plow. With no large draft animals available, peasants used ordinary wooden tacllas to till their land. The ornate ceremonial taclla replica at right bears a jug for chicha *as well as an ear of corn, together indicating the Incas' high regard for the grain that was a source of both food and drink.*

129

conquerors. But now agriculturalists are focusing their attention on other produce commonly consumed in Inca times. Among the long-neglected crops having a resurgence is quinoa, which contains up to 50 percent more protein than rice, wheat, or corn. It is being distributed widely and has begun to appear in American supermarkets. The non-Andean world is also showing interest in *arracacha,* a distant relative of the carrot, which combines the tastes of celery, cabbage, and roasted chestnuts; amaranth, a plant with spinachlike leaves and myriad protein-rich seeds that, when heated, burst open like nutty popcorn; and *nuñas,* a remarkable variety of bean with the flavor of roasted peanuts. Oca, similar to the sweet potato, has become popular in New Zealand, and cherimoya, a fruit once prized by the Incas, is now grown commercially in California.

The proud past is gathering renewed strength in the hearts and minds of young Andeans. Peruvian schoolchildren learn to recite the rhythmical list of rulers of the Inca dynasty, chanting "Manco Capac, Sinchi Roca, Lloque Yupanqui, Mayta Capac, Capac Yupanqui, Inca Roca, Yahuar Huacac, Viracocha, Pachacuti, Topa Inca Yupanqui, Huayna Capac, Huascar, Atahualpa," names that call forth images of a creative, orderly people who became a constructive force of boundless energy and heroic achievements.

LIVING DEAD OF THE ANDES

As early as 4000 BC, there were Andean peoples who mummified their dead. Perhaps they were simply copying nature, since many lived near coastal deserts where corpses resisted decay for millennia, preserved by the arid climate alone. The mummy bundle shown above is one of these, found in 1896 on the Peruvian coast near Lima by the German archaeologist Max Uhle. Within lies a 12-year-old girl, confined in a basket covered by a woven woolen shroud, where she had remained almost intact for more than 500 years. Her family had simply placed her body, carefully wrapped but unembalmed, in extremely dry soil.

Such models of natural preservation bolstered the practice of ancestor worship that took hold as societies grew increasingly complex. Some communities began using artificial techniques to keep the bodies of clan elders or deceased chiefs in a lifelike state. These mummies played a ceremonial role during religious rites. They also enhanced the status of their fortunate possessors, who would consult mummified relatives on practical and moral issues.

Today, Andean mummies speak volumes about the world in which they lived. Some, shipped to high-technology laboratories, have been examined with techniques at the cutting edge of science. In the early 1980s, for example, American forensic scientists, using chemical analyses of hair samples, developed methods for determining whether a person had ingested cocaine. Cocaine is derived from coca leaves, which the Incas chewed to relieve fatigue. Successfully employing these techniques, which were developed for use in law enforcement, a team of four pathologists and an anthropologist tested for traces of coca in the hair of 163 mummies from different regions. They discovered that coca-leaf chewing had been widespread throughout the Andes. The team is continuing the study in order to follow the practice back to its presumed origins in Ecuador, about 3000 BC.

The mummies of a group of Inca emperors and their wives were shown to the early Spanish-Inca chronicler El Inca Garcilaso de la Vega in 1570, leading him to observe: "It must be supposed that they were prepared in some way, for bodies, dead for so many years, could not be so entire, and so covered with flesh, without the application of something to preserve them." He assumed that they had been taken high into the mountains and left for a period of time to dry out in the cold, thin air. He learned from another priest, who had examined the mummies, that bitumen, a tarlike substance, had been used to protect the leathery skin.

Garcilaso's report was only an educated guess, since the Incas never revealed their embalming secrets. What is known is that most of the mummies found, either predating the Incas or under their rule, were natural-ly dried, and that only in a few cultures were artificial methods used. Some early groups deliberately chose burial sites in desert coastal regions or in the dry, high plains. Others assisted nature by curing bodies over a fire. There were peoples who simply eviscerated their corpses; some took the process farther and filled them with plant materials, and others included treatment with resins, oils, and herbs.

Numerous mummies, dating from about AD 400, were found on the south coast of Peru, wrapped in four layers of cotton cloth. One scholar has suggested that each of these shrouds may symbolize a separate burial of the same corpse, reflecting a pre-Inca belief that there were four stages on the deceased's journey to heaven. The layers of fabric that tightly enveloped the cadaver functioned like a wick, drawing off fluids.

The burial style of a bundle indicates the status of the deceased. Regional nobles were interred in multiroom sepulchers with their possessions, and often with their wives, retainers, and slaves. Commoners generally end-ed their days in simple graves in the community's out-lying fields, securely wrapped, surrounded by the few objects of value they had owned in life.

Some 5,000 years ago, on the north coast of Chile, the child above was prepared for burial. After the internal organs were removed, the trunk, arms, and legs were braced with sticks. Coated with clay, the body was then swathed in the skins of birds and topped with a wig made of human hair.

To demonstrate the sizes of his mummy bundles relative to that of a living person, archaeologist Max Uhle posed a workman with two of his finds (above) *during his 1896 dig at*

Pachacamac, on the southern coast of Peru. Like many Andean mummies, these cadavers had been placed in their bales with their legs flexed and drawn up to the chest.

Shell inlays create haunting eyes that stare from the false head attached to a Pachacamac mummy bundle 800 to 1,200 years old. Textiles and feathers form the headdress. Adding such a head, or a mask, gave the packets a more human appearance and enabled the living to relate more comfortably to the dead.

Draped in a cloak of plumes and shod in sandals of wool and leather, this mummified man was 35 years old when he died. His gold adornments, including a crown, earrings of feathered wooden birds, and a mouthpiece decorated with serpents, signify their owner's royal status. He stood five feet, eight inches tall when he lived, sometime between the third and seventh centuries AD.

A stretcher bound to the third shroud (below) reinforced the bundle, making it easier to carry. Its poles, each nearly three feet long, had once served as beams for a so-called backstrap loom, probably belonging to the dead woman.

Bound ▮▮ knotted net bag of plant-fiber rope, the mummy bundle above appears as archaeologist Karen Stothert first saw it. Observing two distinct styles of knotting, she determined that more than one person made the bag.

Lifting the third shroud revealed a cloth parcel, ears of corn, gourds, and several distaffs. Among the contents of the work-basket, in the center, were no fewer than 69 colorfully decorated spindles.

A bowl, painted black (above), and a ceramic figurine (below, left), found in a workbasket within the third shroud, were instrumental in determining the age of the mummy. Their stylistic similarity to well-established Inca artifacts helped the archaeologists deduce that the woman's burial took place during the period of the Inca empire, between 1476 and 1532. Inside the bowl are chunks of a mineral used to fix dyes.

So intricately assembled was the mummy bundle of a woman uncovered near the town of Ancón, Peru, in 1976 that it took the archaeologists Karen Stothert and Rogger Ravines almost two full days to reach the skeleton within. It was a huge bale, weighing more than 150 pounds, buried during the time of the Incas.

By noting what was found in each layer as she carefully removed the four shrouds, Stothert could reconstruct the original burial procedure. Dressed in a sleeveless tunic, the woman had been placed on a large piece of cloth with her head resting on a cotton-stuffed pillow and her bare feet tucked into a cross-legged position. Three rings—two of metal and one of beads—adorned her hands, which were laid across her chest.

Atop her body was a wicker workbasket containing a weaving kit filled with ones of cotton fiber, a wooden bobbin decorated with carved monkeys, 14 painted spindles, a distaff, and various dyestuffs. Small cloth parcels surrounding the corpse held corn, fruits, and beans, eight silver rings, and a *spondylus* shell from Ecuador 700 miles away. A handful of coca leaves had been placed under her chin.

All this had been arranged on the first shroud—a beige fabric with green and maroon stripes—before it was folded tightly across the body and sewn shut. The parcel was then packed with leaves and enclosed inside a second cloth. Again, the bundle was enlarged by the addition of many artifacts, foodstuffs, and a second workbasket. After sealing a third covering, the mourners lashed the great package to a stretcher and swathed it once more. Stothert estimated that it would have taken one person 883 hours to produce the nearly 100 square feet of cloth used to wrap the mummy.

After her trappings were removed, the woman's skeleton appeared. All the flesh was gone, but her skull was still crowned with hair, and between her teeth lay a piece of silver, perhaps to bring her affluence in the afterlife.

ISSUES OF SICKNESS AND HEALTH

Subjected to forensic autopsies, x-rays, and electron microscopes, Andean mummies have yielded surprising information. Samples of their soft tissues, when rehydrated, have even enabled scientists to identify diseases that afflicted the peoples of this region throughout their history. Defying conventional wisdom, mummy studies revealed that when Andean civilization shifted to agriculture, health did not improve but declined. Hunter-gatherers were not stricken with many of the illnesses that plagued their descendants, and early cultures had a child-mortality rate roughly half that of later populations. As nomadic groups settled into sedentary societies, sanitation problems led to an increase in tuberculosis, pneumonia, and intestinal parasites.

Verified also is the terrible toll exacted by European-borne smallpox, measles, typhus, cholera, yellow fever, and bubonic plague—which killed an estimated 95 percent of the Inca population. But a tantalizing question goes unanswered. Was syphilis brought to Europe from America? There is evidence that the organism causing it existed in the New World prior to the Spanish conquest, whereas the disease was unknown in Europe before 1492.

On the new research frontier of molecular archaeology, scientists have found a way to isolate, in the tissues of mummies, DNA—the chromosome molecule that transfers genetic characteristics in all life forms. As they replicate the DNA, these pioneers are looking both for family connections and for kinship among peoples. In so doing, they hope to pinpoint the origins of ethnic communities. The process may also show how some diseases arose.

Lung tissue, 1,300 years old, was taken from this mummified Nazca boy (right), then rehydrated in the laboratory. Bacteria found were tested to reveal that the child had suffered from tuberculosis, which had affected his liver, kidney, and spine, causing the curvature in his back.

The first recorded case of hookworm infestation in the Americas was that of this Tiahuanaco mummy (right), dating from sometime around AD 900. Using a scanning electron microscope, pathologists discovered hookworms attached to the interior of the mummy's small intestine.

It had long been suspected that the Incas practiced human sacrifice after such momentous events as earthquakes or great military victories. Early chroniclers, however, presented contradictory accounts, and scholars hotly debated the question for centuries. Then, archaeologists found indisputable evidence of the fact in a collection of mummies.

Many early Catholic missionaries reported tales of youngsters who were strangled, had their throats slit with an ornate ceremonial knife called a *tumi*, or were left to die of exposure high in the Andes, their deaths assuring community welfare and bringing great honor to their families. Father Bernabé Cobo wrote that 200 children had been sacrificed to celebrate an emperor's coronation. Perhaps it was in reaction to Spanish use of these grisly anecdotes to justify conquest and forced conversion that Garcilaso de la Vega denied that such "barbarian ceremonies" existed among his mother's Inca ancestors.

Only in 1897 did the first solid clues of such rites appear. While excavating a cemetery at the Inca-built sun temple of Pachacamac, Max Uhle found the remains of a group of young women— buried with an array of Inca objects—who "did not die a natural death, but were victims of strangulation." He concluded that they were priestesses of the sun god, Inti, and that they had been ceremonially slain. Then, starting in 1954, a series of finds high in the southern Andes revealed the prowess and dedication that the Incas put into these deadly devotions. At heights that challenge the best-equipped modern expeditions—for example, near the 17,815-foot summit of Chile's Cerro el Plomo and on the Cerro Aconcagua in Argentina—climbers stumbled upon burial chambers holding the richly bedecked bodies of youths, dead for five centuries but perfectly preserved by the year-round cold. Some archaeologists believe that through these mountain sacrifices the Incas combined appeasement of the local mountain deity with worship of Inti, thus gaining respect for their own religion.

At each of these locations, 500 years ago, Inca priests and worshipers, having chosen a highborn youngster of flawless beauty, had walked with the child to a hallowed pinnacle. They carried firewood, stones to build the burial chamber, and artifacts to place in the young victim's grave. Some of the mummies wore expressions of untroubled repose, leading archaeologists to conclude that the youngsters had been first intoxicated with *chicha*, then buried alive. Before the alcoholic stupor faded, they had frozen to death.

Bent in a fetal position, the seven-year-old boy found on Aconcagua was wrapped in a cloak of yellow macaw feathers and several embroidered blankets. His body was painted red, a symbol of life, and he had been dressed in a wool tunic and sandals and adorned with a necklace made of stone beads.

Among the objects found in the grave of the boy of Aconcagua was a diminutive two-inch figure of a male (left) and a small plume (above).

El Plomo's eight-year-old (right) wears a
headdress of condor feathers, an alpaca
cloak, silver ornaments, and red face
paint. Vomit stains his tunic where he
threw up beer given to numb his senses.
Found with him (foreground) were
a bag of coca, figurines of a woman
and two llamas, and pouches of
the youth's own baby teeth,
nail parings, and hair.

A FLOWERING OF CULTURES

Long before the Incas came to dominance, several different cultures flourished in the Andean region. The first hunters and fishers arrived at least 12,000 years ago, and by 3000 BC, fishing villages dotted the arid coast, and small farming communities were springing up in the desert oases and in the fertile valleys of the Andean foothills.

A millennium later, larger social groupings moved inland, over the peaks, settling on the forested eastern slopes and using irrigation methods that had been developed on the coast to water their crops. Population centers grew up around temple complexes, and artisans began turning out pottery and textiles of increasing sophistication.

Archaeologists classify Andean artifacts by time period and geographical distribution. They use the term *horizons* to identify major phases of stylistic unity, broken down by the similarities that the objects display in their aesthetics and technology.

EARLY HORIZON: 1400-400 BC

STAFF GOD

Named for the temple center at Chavin de Huantar, in a small northern valley on the eastern slopes of the Andes, the Chavin style—tied to a powerful new religion—emerged around 1400 BC and reached the peak of its influence by 400 BC.

Believed to have been focused on an oracle who allegedly could see the future, fight disease, and petition the gods, the religion, or cult, gradually spread south. It reached the area of modern Lima by 1000 BC and Ayacucho, more than 200 miles farther inland, by 500 BC. Priests may have been sent from Chavin de Huantar to teach communities to worship Chavin deities like the feline or staff god *(above)*, so named for the rod he holds.

The Chavin people made several major technological advances. They introduced the loom and experimented with metallurgic techniques, such as soldering, welding, and alloying gold and silver. Among the items they produced were large metal sculptures and yarn-dyed fabrics with painted designs of such icons of the Chavin cult as a god with a grinning jaguar face and animals found in the Amazon lowlands.

EARLY INTERMEDIATE PERIOD: 400 BC-AD 550

MOCHE VESSEL

Distinctive regional styles began to emerge on Peru's southern coast. Two notable features of the so-called Paracas culture of the Paracas Peninsula were its beautiful textiles and its bottle-shaped shaft tombs, each with room for at least 40 bodies.

Another people, the Nazca, farmed valleys 200 miles south of present-day Lima. By 370 BC, a Nazca style dominated the southwestern coast, leaving its mark particularly on ceramics. The Nazca are famous for the puzzling Nazca lines—huge ground drawings made by scraping away stones and gravel to reveal the lighter-colored earth beneath, then piling these stones along the edges. The lines are most likely an expression of the Nazca religion.

On the northern coast of Peru, the warlike Moche culture arose about 100 BC and spread its control more than 150 miles along the coast. The Moche developed a complex metallurgy, monumental buildings made of adobe, and an elaborate art style—expressed significantly in vessels that bear realistic portraits *(above)*.

MIDDLE HORIZON: AD 550-900

STAFF GOD SCULPTURE

Now dawned the age of great cities. At 12,500 feet, on the shores of Lake Titicaca, pyramids and stone temples rose, decorated with fine carvings such as that of the god *(above)* thought to be an interpretation of the old Chavin staff god. The people who built these edifices settled the site around 1000 BC and began to construct the city of Tiahuanaco about AD 100.

By AD 500, the Tiahuanacans dominated the southern Andes, disappearing about 500 years later. During their hegemony they established faraway colonies, reclaimed land from around the shores of Lake Titicaca, and sent llama caravans to trade along the coast.

Meanwhile, Huari, a settlement 600 miles to the north, was growing into a city. At its height it had between 35,000 and 70,000 inhabitants, whose houses were served by an underground water system. Weaving counted as one of the culture's artistic traditions. When the Huari people vanished around AD 900, they left a major legacy—the concept and institutions of the imperial state.

LATE INTERMEDIATE PERIOD (COASTAL): AD 900-1476

GOLDEN TUMI

LATE INTERMEDIATE PERIOD (HIGHLAND): AD 900-1476

KILLKE PITCHER

LATE HORIZON: AD 1476-1532

INCA FIGURE

EARLY COLONIAL PERIOD: AD 1532-1572

PIZARRO PORTRAIT

Collapsing empires ushered in a time of strife as smaller groups, emboldened by the Huari example, tried their hand at empire building. Starting from the former Moche heartland on the northern coast of Peru, the Chimu gradually incorporated 600 miles of coastline into their realm. From Chan Chan, their well-irrigated desert capital of 36,000 inhabitants, the lords of Chimu ruled a society of rigid classes, where highly skilled artisans enjoyed special favor.

The Chimu empire was supported by complex irrigation and enriched by conquest of such neighboring cultures as the Chancay, the Ica-Chinca, and the Sican. Sican art is represented above by a ceremonial knife. At their peak the Chimu adorned their clothing and household articles with intricately worked gold, wove precious textiles of surpassing beauty, and vied for power with their highland Inca rivals.

Descended from a people who had settled in the valley of Cuzco, more than 11,000 feet above sea level, the Incas did not develop a distinctive culture until AD 1200, signified by the pitcher above. Although Cuzco, their capital, had begun to expand, their power remained local. Then, in 1438, Pachacuti Inca Yupanqui took the throne. Calling himself Earthshaker, he marched through the Andes conquering, negotiating, and forging a string of states into a single mighty empire. Pachacuti rebuilt Cuzco into a city of enormous stone palaces and temples and brought his numerous provinces under the direction of a single vast, well-functioning governmental bureaucracy. His son, Topa Inca, succeeded him in 1471, after having dealt the Chimu the defeat that secured Inca sovereignty over the entire region, from Ecuador to the heart of Chile.

Its power secured, the Inca culture soared to its zenith. A vast road system carried armies and rich trade. Goldworking, ceramics, and textiles reached new heights of beauty and technical perfection. Stonecutters executed massive, precision-hewn edifices. Inca nobles, like the one shown above in a golden statuette, ruled the Andes until the emperor Huayna Capac died of smallpox sometime between 1525 and 1527, followed shortly thereafter by his heir, leaving open the question of succession and setting off a civil war. The war ended in 1532 when one of Huayna Capac's two contending sons, Atahualpa, became the victor, and the other, Huascar, a prisoner.

By this time, the Spaniard Francisco Pizarro had made a fateful sighting of the Inca coast. With fewer than 200 men, the conquistador would take advantage of the civil war and smallpox epidemic raging through the empire to attack Inca troops, capture Atahualpa, and execute him.

Pizarro and his band advanced on Cuzco in 1533, and were overwhelmed by the city's unexpected beauty. They placed Manco Inca, Atahualpa's half brother, on the throne to rule as a Spanish puppet.

Soon afterward, Manco Inca led his people in an unsuccessful revolt. He was ultimately forced to flee Cuzco, where Pizarro ruled until he was murdered in 1541 by supporters of a rival. Within the year, a viceroy arrived in Lima to govern the Andean territories as provinces of Spain.

In 1545 the Spanish found and killed Manco Inca, still emperor to a few thousand Incas who had taken refuge with him in the jungle, where they built the city of Vilcabamba. Manco's son, Tupac Amaru, the last Inca emperor, held out until his base in Vilcabamba was overrun by the Spaniards in 1572.

ACKNOWLEDGMENTS

The editors wish to thank the following individuals and institutions for their valuable assistance in the preparation of this volume:

Ferdinand Anton, Munich; Arthur Aufderheide, Department of Pathology, University of Minnesota, School of Medicine, Duluth; Richard L. Burger, Peabody Museum of Natural History, Yale University, New Haven, Connecticut; Eve Cockburn, Paleopathology Association, Detroit, Michigan; Alana Cordy-Collins, Department of Anthropology, University of San Diego, San Diego, California; Christopher B. Donnan, Department of Anthropology, University of California, Los Angeles; Clark L. Erickson, Department of Anthropology/ University Museum, University of Pennsylvania, Philadelphia; Stuart Fleming, University Museum, University of Pennsylvania, Philadelphia; LaCynda Gibson, Andean Explorers Foundation and Ocean Sailing Club, Reno, Nevada; April Goebel, National Geographic Society, Washington, D.C.; Martha Hill, Peabody Museum of Natural History, Yale University, New Haven, Connecticut; J. L. Hollowell, Elkton, Maryland; Heidi Klein, Bildarchiv Preussischer Kulturbesitz, Berlin; Sue McIntyre, Arlington, Virginia; W. Iain Mackay, British Museum, Museum of Mankind, London; Susan A. Niles, Department of Anthropology and Sociology, Lafayette College, Easton, Pennsylvania; Calogero Panepinto, Milan; Lino Pellegrini, Milan; Sara Posey, Department of Ethnography, British Museum, London; Walter Reunig, Museum für Völkerkunde, Munich; Luisa Ricciarini, Milan; Royal Library, Copenhagen; Gene Savoy, Andean Explorers Foundation and Ocean Sailing Club, Reno, Nevada; Axel Schulze-Thulin, Linden-Museum Stuttgart, Stuttgart; Anthony Shelton, Department of Ethnography, Brighton Museum and Art Gallery, East Sussex; Charles Stanish, Department of Anthropology, Field Museum of Natural History, Chicago, Illinois; Karen Stothert, Department of Sociology and Anthropology, Trinity University, San Antonio, Texas; John W. Verano, Department of Anthropology, Smithsonian Institution, Washington, D.C.

PICTURE CREDITS

The sources for the illustrations in this volume are listed below. Credits from left to right are separated by semicolons; credits from top to bottom are separated by dashes.

Cover: Brian Moser/Hutchison Library, London; inset, Museum Rietberg, Zurich. End paper: Art by Paul Breeden. 6: Hans Silvester-RAPHO, Paris—American Museum of Natural History, photo R. P. Sheridan 3211(2). 8, 9: Yale University, Peabody Museum of Natural History, New Haven. 10, 11: Yale University, Peabody Museum of Natural History, New Haven; Yale Peruvian Expedition Papers, Manuscripts and Archives, Yale University Library, New Haven, photographed by William K. Sacco—Yale University, Peabody Museum of Natural History, New Haven. 13: Art by Stephen R. Wagner. 14: Musée de l'Homme, Paris; Thomas Gilcrease Institute of American History and Art, Tulsa. 17: Loren McIntyre, courtesy Museo e Instituto de Arqueología, Universidad de San Antonio Abad del Cuzco. 19-23: Gene Savoy, Andean Explorers Foundation and Ocean Sailing Club, Reno. Map by Gary Robert Buchanan. 27: Loren McIntyre. 28, 29: Photo, John Bigelow Taylor 1991/American Museum of Natural History; Archivo Oronoz, Madrid. 30, 31: Dr. Gordon McEwan/Denver Art Museum. 32: Archivo Oronoz/Museo de America, Madrid 4665. 35: W.P.S./Ricciarini, Milan. 36-38: Yale University, Peabody Museum of Natural History, New Haven. 39: W.P.S./Ricciarini, Milan. 40, 41: Yale University, Peabody Museum of Natural History, New Haven; Luisa Ricciarini, Milan. 42, 43: Yale University, Peabody Museum of Natural History, New Haven; Tom Owen Edmunds, London. 44, 45: W.P.S./Ricciarini, Milan. 46: Loren McIntyre. 48, 49: W.P.S./Ricciarini, Milan. 50: Servicio Aerofotografico Nacional. 51: Art by Stephen R. Wagner. 54: W.P.S./Ricciarini, Milan. 58, 59: Ferdinand Anton, Munich/Museo de la Universidad Cuzco; Det Kongelige Bibliotek, Copenhagen; Musée de l'Homme, Paris, photo D. Destable. 60: Neil Maurer—Foto Ferdinand Anton, Munich, private collection; from *Circa 1492: Art in the Age of Exploration,* Jay A. Levenson, editor, National Gallery of Art, Yale University Press, New Haven, 1991. 61: Dumbarton Oaks Research Library and Collections, Washington, D.C. 62: Loren McIntyre. 63: American Museum of Natural History, photo D. Finnin. 66, 67: Loren McIntyre/Amano Museum, Lima. 68, 69: Det Kongelige Bibliotek, Copenhagen. 71: Loren McIntyre/Museo e Instituto de Arqueología, Universidad de San Antonio Abad del Cuzco. 72, 73: Det Kongelige Bibliotek, Copenhagen. 75: W.P.S./Ricciarini, Milan. 76, 77: Background from *Inca Architecture* by Graziano Gasparini and Luise Margolies, Indiana University Press, Bloomington, 1980. Daniele Pellegrini, Milan (2)—Robert Harding Picture Library, London; Luisa Ricciarini, Milan. 78, 79: Background from *Inca Architecture* by Graziano Gasparini and Luise Margolies, Indiana University Press, Bloomington, 1980. Dr. Gordon McEwan/Denver Art

Museum (2). 80, 81: Background from *Inca Architecture* by Graziano Gasparini and Luise Margolies, Indiana University Press, Bloomington, 1980. ZEFA, London; © Wolfgang Kaehler. 82, 83: Background from *Inca Architecture* by Graziano Gasparini and Luise Margolies, Indiana University Press, Bloomington, 1980. W.P.S./Ricciarini, Milan; © Wolfgang Kaehler—Robert Harding Picture Library, London. 84: Loren McIntyre/Museo del Oro del Peru, Lima. 86, 87: Neg. no. 334600, courtesy Dept. of Library Services, American Museum of Natural History. 88-89: Ullstein Bilderdienst, Berlin—Johan Reinhard, La Paz, Bolivia. 90: Nicole Couture/University of Chicago, Dept. of Anthropology. 91: Flip Schulke/Black Star. 92, 93: All John W. Verano, except far left, Loren McIntyre/Museo e Instituto de Arqueología, Universidad de San Antonio Abad del Cuzco. 94, 95: Dumbarton Oaks Research Library and Collections, Washington, D.C.; Dr. Gordon McEwan, courtesy S.A.N. Peru; Art Studio, Milan. 96: Hans Silvester-RAPHO, Paris; art by Stephen R. Wagner. 98: Dr. Gordon McEwan/Denver Art Museum. 99: Loren McIntyre. 100, 101: Neg. no. 334811, courtesy American Museum of Natural History, photo George Johnson. 102: Dr. James S. Kus, Fresno—Dr. Gordon McEwan/Denver Art Museum. 103: John B. Powell—Dr. Gordon McEwan/Denver Art Museum. 104, 105: Dr. Elias Mujica—Loren McIntyre. 106: Francisco Hidalgo, Paris. 107: Metropolitan Museum of Art, Michael C. Rockefeller Memorial Collection, gift of Nelson A. Rockefeller, 1969, 1978.412.219 and 1978.412.160; far right, Lee Boltin. 108: Loren McIntyre/Museum e Instituto de Arqueología, Universidad de San Antonio Abad del Cuzco; from "Inka-Peru" (Vol. 2 of 1991 catalog), M.R.A.H. Brussels AAM 46.7.286. 109: Francisco Hidalgo, Paris; Bildarchiv Hansmann, Munich. 111: Michael Holford, London. 112, 113: Art by Stephen R. Wagner; © 1982 David L. Brill. 114, 115: Christopher B. Donnan; Michael E. Moseley (2)—G. Dagli Orti, Paris. 116, 117: Trans. no. 2574(2) (photo by Richard P. Sheridan), courtesy Dept. of Library Services, American Museum of Natural History—Alana Cordy-Collins; G. Dagli Orti, Paris (2). 118: Don Bleitz; Textile Museum, Washington, D.C. 119: Trans. no. 3420(2) (photo by Beckett/Hollembeak), courtesy Dept. of Library Services, American Museum of Natural History—Textile Museum, Washington, D.C., 91.729. 120, 121: Foto Ferdinand Anton, Munich/Museo de Oro, Miguel Mujica Gallo Foundation, Lima; Francisco Hidalgo, Paris (2). 122: Loren McIntyre. 125: Neil Maurer. 126: Linden-Museum Stuttgart, photo Ursula Didoni. 127: Art Institute of Chicago/photo by Robert Hashimoto. 128: Loren McIntyre/Garcilazo (Cuzco) (2). 129: Loren McIntyre/Amano Museum, Lima; Det Kongelige Bibliotek, Copenhagen. 130: Det Kongelige Bibliotek, Copenhagen. 132, 133: Dr. Gordon McEwan/Denver Art Museum; Derek Bayes/courtesy of the Trustees of the British Museum, Dept. of Ethnography; Loren McIntyre/Amano Museum; photo H. R. Dorig/Hutchison Library, London. 134: Photo H. R. Dorig/Hutchison Library, London (2). 136: Denver Art Museum. 137: Peabody Museum of Archaeology and Ethnology, Harvard University, photo by Hillel Burger—Neil Maurer. 138, 139: Loren McIntyre. 140: Daniele Pellegrini, Milan. 141: Wolfgang Kaehler Photography. 143: Art by Stephen R. Wagner—Dr. Gordon McEwan/Denver Art Museum (2). 144, 145: Denver Art Museum—Craig Morris, New York City—Linden-Museum Stuttgart, photo Ursula Didoni. 147: Dr. Gordon McEwan/Denver Art Museum. 149: University Museum, University of Pennsylvania, neg. no. T4-131c3. 150: American Museum of Natural History, photo by R. P. Sheridan 2647(2); University Museum, University of Pennsylvania, neg. no. G5-18588. 151: American Museum of Natural History, photo by C. Chesek, cat. no. B/7737; from "L'Or du Pérou," Fondation de l'Hermitage, Lausanne, 17 Juin-4 Septembre, 1988, photos by Francisco Hidalgo. 152, 153: Neil Maurer. 154, 155: Eve Cockburn. 156: Juan Schobinger. 157: Loren McIntyre/Chile's Natural History Museum, Quinta Normol, Santiago. 158, 159: Art by Paul Breeden.

BIBLIOGRAPHY

BOOKS

Adorno, Rolena. *Guaman Poma.* Austin: University of Texas Press, 1986.

Anton, Ferdinand. *The Art of Ancient Peru.* New York: G. P. Putnam's Sons, 1972.

Ascher, Marcia, and Robert Ascher. *Code of the Quipu.* Ann Arbor: University of Michigan Press, 1981.

Baudin, Louis. *Daily Life in Peru.* Translated by Winifred Bradford. New York: Macmillan, 1962.

Beals, Carleton. *Nomads and Empire Builders.* Philadelphia: Chilton Company, Book Division, 1961.

Beltrán, Miriam. *Cuzco: Window on Peru* (2d ed., rev.). New York: Alfred A. Knopf, 1970.

Bennett, Ross S. (Ed.). *Lost Empires: Living Tribes.* Washington, D.C.: National Geographic Society, 1982.

Bingham, Alfred M. *Portrait of an Explorer: Hiram Bingham, Discoverer of Machu Picchu.* Ames: Iowa

State University Press, 1989.

Bingham, Hiram. *Lost City of the Incas: The Story of Machu Picchu and Its Builders*. New York: Atheneum, 1971.

Brundage, Burr Cartwright. *Empire of the Inca*. Norman: University of Oklahoma Press, 1963.

Cieza de León, Pedro de. *The Incas*. Translated by Harriet de Onis, edited by Victor Wolfgang von Hagen. Norman: University of Oklahoma Press, 1959.

Cobo, Bernabé:
History of the Inca Empire. Edited and translated by Roland Hamilton. Austin: University of Texas Press, 1979.
Inca Religion and Customs. Edited and translated by Roland Hamilton. Austin: University of Texas Press, 1990.

Cockburn, Aidan, and Eve Cockburn (Eds.). *Mummies, Disease, and Ancient Cultures* (abridged ed.). Cambridge: Cambridge University Press, 1980.

Coe, Michael, Dean Snow, and Elizabeth Benson. *Atlas of Ancient America*. New York: Facts On File, 1989.

Cotterell, Arthur (Ed.). *The Encyclopedia of Ancient Civilizations*. London: Penguin Books, 1988.

Cottrell, Leonard. *Digs and Diggers: A Book of World Archaeology*. Cleveland: World Publishing Company, 1964.

Deuel, Leo. *Conquistadors without Swords: Archaeologists in the Americas*. New York: St. Martin's Press, 1967.

Disselhoff, Dietrich. *Daily Life in Ancient Peru*. Translated by Alisa Jaffa. New York: McGraw-Hill, 1967.

Engel, Frederic André. *An Ancient World Preserved*. New York: Crown Publishers, 1976.

The European Emergence: TimeFrame AD 1500-1600 (Time Frame series). Alexandria, Va.: Time-Life Books, 1989.

Garcilaso de la Vega. *The Incas: The Royal Commentaries of the Inca*. Translated by Marìa Jolas from the French edition, Alain Gheerbrant, editor. New York: Avon Books, 1971.

Gasparini, Graziano, and Luise Margolies. *Inca Architecture*. Translated by Patricia J. Lyon. Bloomington: Indiana University Press, 1980.

Hagen, Victor Wolfgang von. *The Desert Kingdoms of Peru*. Greenwich, Conn.: New York Graphic Society Publishers, 1965.

Hardoy, Jorge E. *Pre-Columbian Cities*. New York: Walker and Company, 1973.

Hawkes, Jacquetta (Ed.). *Atlas of Ancient Archaeology*. New York: McGraw-Hill, 1974.

Hemming, John:
The Conquest of the Incas. New York: Harcourt Brace Jovanovich, 1970.
Machu Picchu. New York: Newsweek Book Division, 1981.
Monuments of the Incas. Boston: Little, Brown and Company, 1982.

Huamán Poma de Ayala, Felipe de: *Letter to a King*. New York: E. P. Dutton, 1978.
Nuevo Corónica y Buen Gobierno. Edited by Richard Pietschmann. Paris: Institute d'Ethnologie, 1936.

Hyams, Edward, and George Ordish. *The Last of the Incas*. New York: Simon and Schuster, 1963.

Hyslop, John. *Inka Settlement Planning*. Austin: University of Texas Press, 1990.

Jackson, Donald Dale, and the Editors of Time-Life Books. *The Explorers* (The Epic of Flight series). Alexandria, Va.: Time-Life Books, 1983.

Katz, Friedrich. *The Ancient American Civilizations*. Translated by K. M. Lois Simpson. New York: Praeger Publishers, 1974.

Kendall, Ann. *Everyday Life of the Incas*. New York: Dorset Press, 1973.

The Land of the Incas. Photographs by Hans Silvester, text by Jacques Soustelle. Translated by Jane Brenton. London: Thames and Hudson, 1986.

Lanning, Edward P. *Peru before the Incas*. Englewood Cliffs, N.J.: Prentice-Hall, 1967.

Leonard, Jonathan Norton, and the Editors of Time-Life Books. *Ancient America* (Great Ages of Man series). New York: Time Inc., 1967.

Lewis, Brenda Ralph. *Growing Up in Inca Times*. London: Batsford Academic and Educational Limited, 1981.

Lumbreras, Luis G. *The Peoples and Cultures of Ancient Peru*. Translated by Betty J. Meggers. Washington, D.C.: Smithsonian Institution Press, 1974.

McIntyre, Loren. *The Incredible Incas and Their Timeless Land*. Washington, D.C.: National Geographic Society, 1975.

McKern, Sharon S. *Exploring the Unknown: Mysteries in American Archaeology*. New York: Praeger Publishers, 1972.

Marrin, Albert. *Inca & Spaniard: Pizarro and the Conquest of Peru*. New York: Atheneum, 1989.

Menzel, Dorothy. *The Archaeology of Ancient Peru and the Work of Max Uhle*. Berkeley: University of California, 1977.

Métraux, Alfred. *The History of the Incas*. Translated by George Ordish. New York: Schocken Books, 1970.

Morris, Craig, and Donald E. Thompson. *Huánuco Pampa*. London: Thames and Hudson, 1985.

Moseley, Michael E., and Kent C. Day (Eds.). *Chan Chan: Andean Desert City*. Albuquerque: University of New Mexico Press, 1982.

Murra, John Victor. *The Economic Organization of the Inka State* (Research in Economic Anthropology, Supplement 1). Greenwich, Conn.: JAI Press, 1980.

Niles, Susan A. *Callachaca: Style and Status in an Inca Community*. Iowa City: University of Iowa Press, 1987.

Oro del Peru. Photographs by Francisco Hidalgo, text by Aurelio Miro Quesada S. Banco de Lima and Editions Delroisse, 1981.

Parker, Geoffrey (Ed.). *The World: An Illustrated History*. London: Times Books, 1986.

Prescott, William H. *History of the Conquest of Mexico and History of the Conquest of Peru*. New York: Modern Library, n.d.

Reader's Digest. *Mysteries of the Ancient Americas*. Pleasantville, N.Y.: Reader's Digest Association, 1986.

Romé, Jésus, and Lucienne Romé. *Life of the Incas in Ancient Peru*. Translated by Peter J. Tallon. Barcelona: Editions Minerva, 1978.

Rowe, Ann Pollard. *Costumes & Featherwork of the Lords of Chimor*. Washington, D.C.: Textile Museum, 1984.

Rowe, John Howland. *Max Uhle, 1856-1944: A Memoir of the Father of Peruvian Archaeology*. Berkeley: University of California Press, 1954.

Rowe, John Howland, and Dorothy Menzel. *Peruvian Archaeology*. Palo Alto, Calif.: Peek Publications, n.d.

Savoy, Gene. *Antisuyo: The Search for the Lost Cities of the Amazon*. New York: Simon and Schuster, 1970.

Silverblatt, Irene. *Moon, Sun, and Witches*. Princeton: Princeton University Press, 1987.

Stierlin, Henri. *Art of the Incas and Its Origins*. Translated by Betty Ross and Peter Ross. New York: Rizzoli, 1984.

Stuart, George E., and Gene S. Stuart. *Discovering Man's Past in the Americas*. Washington, D.C.: National Geographic Society, 1973.

Viola, Herman J., and Carolyn Margolis (Eds.). *Seeds of Change*. Washington, D.C.: Smithsonian Institution, 1991.

Voyages of Discovery: TimeFrame AD 1400-1500 (Time Frame series). Alexandria, Va.: Time-Life Books, 1989.

Westwood, Jennifer (Ed.). *The Atlas of Mysterious Places*. New York: Weidenfeld & Nicolson, 1987.

Wurster, Wolfgang W. *Die Schatz-Gräber*. Hamburg: GEO, 1991.

PERIODICALS

Allison, Marvin J., Daniel Mendoza, and Alejandro Pezzia. "Documentation of a Case of Tuberculosis in Pre-Columbian America." *American Review of Respiratory Disease*, 1973, Vol. 107.

Allison, Marvin J., et al. "Case of Hookworm Infestation in a Precolumbian American." *American Journal of Physical Anthropology*, July 1974.

Angier, Natalie. "A 'Lost City' Revisited." *Time*, February 11, 1985.

Bingham, Hiram:
"Further Explorations in the Land of the Incas." *National Geographic*, May 1916.
"The Story of Machu Picchu." *National Geographic*, February 1915.

Bray, Warwick. "Agricultural Renascence in the High Andes." *Nature*, May 31, 1990.

Cartmell, Larry W., et al. "The Frequency and Antiquity of Prehistoric Coca-Leaf-Chewing Practices in Northern Chile: Radioimmunoassay of a Cocaine Metabolite in Human-Mummy Hair." *Latin American Antiquity*, 1991, Vol. 2, no. 2.

Denevan, William M. "Peru's Agricultural Legacy." *Focus*, April 1985.

Erickson, Clark L. "Raised Field Agriculture in the Lake Titicaca Basin." *Expedition*, 1988, Vol. 30, no. 3.

Fleming, S. J., and Kathleen Ryan (Eds.). "The Mummies of Pachacamac, Peru." *Masca Journal* (University of Pennsylvania), 1983, Vol. 2, no. 5.

Hagman, Harvey:
"The 'Cloud People' of Old Peru." *Washington Times*, June 6, 1989.
"Site of Ancient City Discovered in Peru." *Washington Times*, September 3, 1989.

Hyslop, John. "Investigating Inca Roads." *Americas*, May/June 1986.

"If You Died in Old Peru." *Natural History*, February 1938.

Keatinge, Richard W., and Kent C. Day. "Chan Chan: A Study of Precolumbian Urbanism and the Management of Land and Water Resources in Peru." *Archaeology*, October 1974.

Key, Hopemary Ann. "Ancient Surgery: No 'Holes' Barred." *Pacific Discovery*, Spring 1991.

"Lost and Found in the Andes." *Discover*, April 1985.

"The Lost City." *Time*, August 28, 1964.

McIntyre, Loren M.:
"The High Andes." *National Geographic*, April 1987.
"Lost Empire of the Incas." *National Geographic*, December 1973.

"The Mist Lifts in the Andes." *Newsweek*, February 11, 1985.

Moseley, Michael E.:
"Chan Chan: Andean Alternative of the Preindustrial City." *Science*, January 1975.
"Peru's Ancient City of Kings." *National Geographic*, March 1973.

Murra, John V.:
"Guaman Poma de Ayala." *Natural History*, September-October 1961.

Ortloff, Charles R. "Canal Builders of Pre-Inca Peru." *Scientific American*, December 1988.

Petrich, Perla. "The Return of the Inca." *UNESCO Courier*, February 1990.

Protzen, Jean-Pierre. "Inca Stonemasonry." *Scientific American*, February 1986.

Roberts, Shauna S. "Molecular Archaeology: PCR Amplifies the Pace of Discovery." *Journal of NIH Research*, September/October 1989.

Rogan, Peter K., and Joseph J. Salvo. "Molecular Genetics of Pre-Columbian South American Mummies." *Molecular Evolution*, 1990, pp. 223-234.

Ruiz, Jesús F. Garcia. "A Labyrinth of Forms." *UNESCO Courier*, July 1984.

Sattaur, Omar. "The Lost Art of the Waru Waru." *New Scientist*, May 12, 1988.

Schobinger, Juan. "Sacrifices of the High Andes." *Natural History*, April 1991.

"Skullduggery." *Scientific American*, June 1990.

Stevens, William K. "Scientists Revive a Lost Secret of Farming." *Science Times*, November 22, 1988.

Stothert, Karen E.:
"Corrections for the Published Descriptions of a Late Horizon Mummy Bundle from Ancon." *Ñawpa Pacha* (Institute of Andean Studies, Berkeley, Calif.), 1991, no. 19.
"Preparing a Mummy Bundle: Note on a Late Burial from An-

con, Peru." *Ñawpa Pacha* (Institute of Andean Studies, Berkeley, Calif.), 1978, no. 16. "Unwrapping an Inca Mummy Bundle." *Archaeology,* July/August 1979.

Vietmeyer, Noel. "Gift of the Incas." *National Wildlife,* September/October 1984.

OTHER PUBLICATIONS

"The Andean Civilizations" (Vol. 2 of *Handbook of South American Indians,* edited by Julian H. Steward). Smithsonian Institution, Bureau of American Ethnology, Bulletin 143. Washington, D.C.: U.S. Government Printing Office, 1946.

Bauer, Brian S., and Charles Stanish. "Killke and Killke-Related Pottery from Cuzco, Peru, in the Field Museum of Natural History." *Fieldiana: Anthropology,* December 1990, no. 15.

Circa 1492: Art in the Age of Exploration. Edited by Jay A. Levenson. Catalog of an exhibition at the National Gallery of Art, Washington, D.C., October 12, 1991-January 12, 1992. New Haven: Yale University Press, 1991.

"Fabric of the Inca Empire: Traditions Suppressed by the European Invasion." Catalog of exhibition, July 13, 1991-January 5, 1992. Washington, D.C.: Textile Museum, 1992.

Hollowell, J. L. "Precision Cutting and Fitting of Stone in Prehistoric Andean Walls: Re-assessment of the Fortaleza, Ollantaytambo, Peru." Unpublished manuscript.

"Inka Peru: Indianische Hochkulturen durch Drei Jahrtausende"

(Vol. 2). Catalog of exhibition at Schlossmuseum Linz, May 12-December 8, 1991. Linz, Austria: Landesmuseum Linz, 1991.

"L'Or du Pérou." Catalog of exhibition at Fondation de l'Hermitage, Lausanne, Switzerland, June 17-September 4, 1988. Lausanne: Fondation de l'Hermitage, 1988.

Lothrop, S. K. "Inca Treasure." Los Angeles, 1938.

McEwan, Gordon. "An Introduction to Andean Art and Archaeology." Manuscript in possession of author, 1990.

Moseley, Michael E. "Peru's Golden Treasures: An Essay on Five Ancient Styles." Chicago: Field Museum of Natural History, 1978.

Michael E. Moseley, and Alana Cordy-Collins (Eds.). *The Northern Dynasties: Kingship and Statecraft in Chimor.* Proceedings of symposium held at Dumbarton Oaks, Washington, D.C., October 12 and 13, 1985. Washington, D.C.: Dumbarton Oaks Research Library and Collections, 1990.

Oro del Perù. Catalog of exhibition at the Palazzo dei Conservatori, Rome, November 1981-January 1982. Milan: Electa, 1981.

"Researchers Seek Understanding of Ancient Surgery." Press release, Smithsonian News Service, March 1990.

Sweat of the Sun, Tears of the Moon: Gold and Emerald Treasures of Colombia. Essays published in conjunction with exhibition at the Natural History Museum of Los Angeles County, July 4-September 6, 1981. Los Angeles: TERRA Magazine Publications, 1981.

MUSEUMS
Readers interested in viewing Inca objects will find outstanding collections in the following institutions.

EUROPE
Linden-Museum Stuttgart, Stuttgart
Museum für Völkerkunde, Berlin
Museum für Völkerkunde, Frankfurt
Rautenstrauch-Joest-Museum, Cologne
Rijksmuseum voor Volkenkunde, Leiden
Roemer- und Pelizaeus-Museum, Hildesheim
Staatliches Museum für Völkerkunde, Munich

PERU
Museo Arqueológico, Cuzco
Museo del Banco Central de Reserva, Lima
Museo del Oro del Peru, Lima
Museo Nacional de Antropología y Arqueología, Lima
Museo Nacional de la Cultura Peruana, Lima

UNITED STATES
American Museum of Natural History, New York
Art Institute of Chicago, Chicago
Brooklyn Museum, Brooklyn
Denver Art Museum, Denver
Dumbarton Oaks Research Library and Collections, Washington, D.C.
Metropolitan Museum of Art, New York
Peabody Museum of Archaeology and Ethnology, Cambridge
Textile Museum, Washington, D.C.
Thomas Gilcrease Institute of American History and Art, Tulsa

INDEX

Amazon River

GATE OF THE SUN

ARYBALLO

EL TORREÓN

Quito

Lake Titicaca

Urubamba River

Ollantaytambo
Tiahuanaco

Vilcabamba
Cuzco

Apurímac River
Machu Picchu

ANDES MOUNTAINS

Huánuco

Tumbes
Cajamarca
Huari

Chan Chan
Ancón
Pachacamac
Nazca

(Lima)

SPANISH SHIP

GOLDEN BIRD

DEATH MASK

PACIFIC OCEAN

N

W   E

S